WHAT TO SAY IN EVERY JOB INTERVIEW

WHAT TO SAY IN EVERY JOB INTERVIEW

HOW TO UNDERSTAND WHAT MANAGERS ARE *REALLY* ASKING AND GIVE THE ANSWERS THAT LAND THE JOB

CAROLE MARTIN

New York   Chicago   San Francisco   Athens   London
Madrid   Mexico City   Milan   New Delhi
Singapore   Sydney   Toronto

1 2 3 4 5 6 7 8 9 0   QFR/QFR   1 0 9 8 7 6 5 4 3

ISBN   978-0-07-181800-1
MHID   0-07-181800-6

e-ISBN   978-0-07-181801-8
e-MHID   0-07-181801-4

Library of Congress Cataloging-in-Publication Data

Martin, Carole
   What to say in every job interview: how to understand what managers are really asking and give the answers that land the job / Carole Martin.
     pages cm
   ISBN-13: 978-0-07-181800-1 (pbk. : alk. paper)
   ISBN-10: 0-07-181800-6 (pbk. : alk. paper)   1. Employment interviewing.
   2. Interviewing.   I. Title.
   HF5549.5.I6M3165 2014
   650.14'4—dc23   2013032593

McGraw-Hill Education books are available at special quantity discounts to use as premiums and sales promotions or for use in corporate training programs. To contact a representative, please visit the Contact Us pages at www.mhprofessional.com.

To Marv—as in "Marvelous"—the best!

To my clients, who continue to keep me on my toes.
Thanks for being my best source of learning.

Contents

Acknowledgments

Many thanks to the great staff at McGraw-Hill for producing wonderful books from my writing. Special thanks to my "shepherd," Casie Vogel, who was with me from the start to the completion of this book. I very much appreciate your faith in me.

Introduction

You've been preparing for your interviews. You've been reading books about interview questions and answers and you've been practicing—you're still not getting the results you want. What's not working for you? Why aren't you getting invited back for a second interview? Why haven't you received a job offer? What can you do to improve your chances in this competitive job market?

There may not be simple answers to those questions, but one thing is for sure: if you continue doing the same thing over and over and continue to get the same results, nothing is going to change. (Albert Einstein described this repetitious pattern of behavior as the definition of "insanity.")

If you want different results to happen, something has to change. This would be a good time to start thinking out of the box and change the way you've been preparing for your interviews. If you are willing to let go of what you've been doing, and are now willing to try something new, this is the book for you.

The purpose of this book is to demonstrate a new technique; a technique that teaches you how to think beyond the questions and answers as the only way to prepare for an interview. By learning to "read between the lines," this book will show you how to think like an interviewer thinks. You can stop worrying about the questions being asked, and start thinking about the concerns behind the questions.

Using this book to prepare for your interviews will introduce you to a new approach and way to think about the interview. Up until now, the preparation has focused on the questions that may or may not be asked by an interviewer. In this book, I will introduce you to a new method of preparation. Using the methodology that I have been using with thousands of clients over the past 15 years, I will share the tools and techniques that have successfully worked for others. The technique is to focus on the key factors of the job as the basis for the interview preparation so that you can answer any question the interviewer asks.

Fear of Questions

In an informal survey, some colleagues found that most candidates have one fear in common about the job interview: the fear that they will not have the answers to the questions that could be asked. Most candidates continue to think of the interview as a test with right or wrong answers. There are no right or wrong answers, but some answers are definitely stronger and some weaker than others; some are downright killers.

The method used in this book is to focus on the factors of the job rather than on the questions and answers. By identifying the key factors, and what is behind the interviewer's questions, you will have a better idea of what the interviewer is looking for in a candidate. For example, if interviewers ask you, "What are your goals?" are they interested in your goals or are they asking how long you are going to stick around? They are probably interested in the latter. They will be listening during the interview to hear why you are interviewing for this particular job. Are you looking for this job as a quick fix? Or, are you really interested in what this particular company does and in the company's mission statement?

By reading between the lines of what the interviewer is asking, you will be able to give him or her an answer to the question that is really being asked. Begin to think, What is really behind the question being asked? What does the interviewer really want to know about me? There is more than likely always another reason that the question is being asked— the hidden meaning behind the question.

A Change in Thinking Equals a New View

The first step on the way to change is to visit a bookstore. The bookstore can be online or an actual store. If you search under the category of Career Books, you will find a wide variety of books on the subject of job interviews. Many of these books deal with questions and answers: *101 Smart Questions, 101 Great Answers, 201 Best Questions to Ask, 301 Smart Answers, How to Ace the Interviewer's Questions*, and the list goes on and on. These books work well if you are focusing only on the questions and answers that take place in an interview. The problem is that you don't know what questions will be asked in the interview, or what the interviewer is looking for.

If you are really ready to try something new and change your thinking, this book is a good place to start. Stop thinking about the questions and answers only and begin thinking about why the interviewer is asking the question. In other words, what's the interviewer really looking for in your answer?

Answers Based on Factors

This new process will require you to study each job posting or job description that you are interested in pursuing and analyze what it will take to do the job successfully. Your task will be to figure out what factors are being sought.

Factor is the term that will be used in this book to describe the key abilities and traits needed to perform the job. You may have seen these factors referred to in other books, or in job postings, by other names such as core competencies, critical skills, or dimensions, to name a few. They all deal with the same principle but just use different words.

The factors are sometimes spelled out for you and easy to work with, while other times you will have to dig to discover them. Sometimes you'll have to read between the lines. By looking at each factor and what it entails you will have a stronger base to start your preparation. If you can demonstrate through your answers that you have the desired qualities and abilities, and even some past experiences, you will begin to be of special interest to the interviewer as the right person for the job.

There will be exercises to work on as a part of your preparation for using the factors as your base. It isn't until you can identify the factors yourself that you can achieve the skill to perform the task.

Letting the Interviewer Know Who You Are

One of the key questions the interviewer is asking himself during the interview is, "Do I want to work with this person? Will this candidate fit in as part of the team?" A primary mistake that many candidates make going into an interview is to try to be someone other than themselves. If you try to impress interviewers by being someone else, you could be making a huge mistake and giving the wrong impression of who you are and what you are capable of doing in a job.

In Chapter 5 of this book, there will be exercises to help you answer that dreaded question: "Tell me about yourself." The answer to this question can set the tone for the rest of the interview. This question will also give you the opportunity to incorporate the key factors into your response.

Walking through the process will assist you in becoming a savvy interviewee. You will be able to stop worrying about the questions and focus on the factors that the interviewer will be focusing on. By breaking the chapters of the book into categories, we will cover all of the topics mentioned.

The Three Main Concerns of the Interviewer

There are three primary concerns going on in interviews. The interviewer wants to know:

1. Can this candidate do the job?
2. Will this candidate "fit" into the department? The company culture?
3. Can we afford the candidate?

Chapters 2, 3, and 4 of the book will cover these categories with specific sections to break down what you will need to deal with these concerns.

Although the criteria will differ from job to job, from field to field, and from industry to industry, these concerns are more or less consistent as a basis of what the interviewer is seeking. As you can see, some of the concerns are more subjective than others. No matter how hard you try, there is a certain amount of subjectivity and likeability in any meeting between people, especially the job interview, where you are being evaluated. The more the interviewer gets to know you as a person and what you have to offer, the more convinced he or she will be that "you can do the job," and that "you will fit in" with the team and the culture or work environment of the company.

The book also covers the question of whether you are "affordable" as a candidate by giving you tools and methods of talking about salary more confidently. Money is one of the most difficult subjects to deal with in any situation, and in interviews it can be twice as painful.

Behavioral Interviewing

An interview technique that is becoming more and more accepted by companies is *behavioral interviewing*. We will cover behavioral style interviewing in Chapter 6. Behavioral questions seek examples or stories about your past behavior as an indicator of your future success. In other words, if you can prove through an example that you have done whatever it is you have said or written about yourself, the interviewer will have proof that you can do what you say you can do.

The interviewer is trying to see a clear picture of who you are, and he can get a better picture of you through your stories and your patterns of behavior.

When you are asked a question that begins with the words: "Give me an example ..." or "Tell me about a time when ..." you are being asked a behavioral question. The premise behind the behavioral question is that if you can prove through your example or story that you have successfully done something before, chances are that you will repeat that behavior again. This type of question solicits far more information for the interviewer than the questions that can be answered with one or two words or a hypothetical answer. Unfortunately, the behavioral interview puts the burden on the candidate to come up with examples of past experiences.

There is no way to accurately predict the questions that will be asked in an interview, but by focusing on the key factors you can prepare before the interview and feel more confident about the process. By taking the time to prepare for each job individually, and by using the factors as a guide, you will have a better idea of what's behind the interviewer's question and be ready with your own stories to convince the interviewer that you are the best person for the job.

The following sections will give you tools and techniques to use to write your examples or stories related to the various factors. You will build and organize an inventory of stories to pull from and use as proof that you have had the experiences you claim you've had.

In Chapter 8, the book will deal with the five categories of questions asked in most interviews. By categorizing these questions, the task of being prepared for all the questions you might be asked becomes more "doable." You will use the factors that you have identified to blend your stories and experiences into the categories instead of memorizing hundreds of questions and answers.

Finally, Chapter 9 of the book will provide a quiz that will help you practice thinking factor first, question second.

There are certain situations in an interview that will be out of your control. You will have to let go of those things. What you can control is your confidence and demeanor. The more confident and prepared you are for the interview, the better your chances will be of impressing the interviewer and convincing him or her that you are the right person for the job. Preparation will improve confidence. Confidence will improve your interviews. Improved interviews will result in more success and possible offers.

Join me on the journey to a new way of thinking about job interviews. I will show you how to think "factor," as well as what's behind the questions being asked by the interviewer. This will give you an edge over the other candidates.

Are you ready to begin?

It's time for a change!

CHAPTER 1

The Key Factors

The Purpose of This Book

The purpose of this book is to demonstrate a new technique: to think beyond the questions and answers as the only way to prepare for an interview. By learning to "read between the lines," this book will show you how to think like an interviewer. You can stop worrying about the question being asked, and start thinking about the concern behind the question.

How Is This Book Different?

The methodology used in this book is a way of preparing for the interview by focusing on the required *factors* of the job as the basis for preparation rather than focusing on the questions that may or may not be asked. I have been using this method of interview preparation for the past 15 years with thousands of clients who consistently send me feedback on the great interview results they've had. The method is simple enough: instead of focusing on the questions, we focus on the key *factors* needed to do the job, and why the interviewer is asking the question. In other words, what's behind

1

the interviewer's question? This method of preparation takes more effort because you will approach each job as a new project that has its own specific factors. By identifying these key factors and revealing what is behind the interviewer's questions, you will have a better idea of what the interviewer is looking for in a candidate.

The best way to leverage these identified factors is by brainstorming and writing stories to use in your interview based on them. Ultimately, you will be more prepared and confident in letting the interviewer know not only that you can do the job, but that you are the right person for the job. The best and only way to let the interviewer know you can do the job is to first have an understanding of the job and what the interviewer is looking for in the ideal candidate.

The Three Main Concerns in Interviews

In this book, we will look at the concerns from the *interviewer's point of view* as well as from *your point of view*. The three main concerns listed below will be covered in-depth in Chapters 2, 3, and 4 of this book.

Concern 1: "Can he or she do the job?" Your job in an interview is to show the interviewer that you can "do the job." There are three categories of skills you need to do just that: *knowledge-based skills, transferable skills,* and *personal traits.* Combined, these skills and traits identify you as an individual and are a part of your personal brand. They make you stand out to an interviewer as a person who has what it takes to perform the job.

Concern 2: "Do we like this candidate? Will he or she fit in?" Although this concern is somewhat out of your control, it is your job to believe in yourself as the best person for this job. There will be no place for false modesty here. If the interviewers do not get to know you, they won't know if you are a person they want to be part of their team. Chapter 3 of this book will help you prepare to help the interviewer get to know you, "the person."

Concern 3: "Can we afford this candidate?" Money is a factor in any business transaction, and the interview, or hiring process, is no exception. Salary issues during the interview and how to deal with the sensitive questions about money will be covered in-depth in Chapter 4 of this book.

Proper Preparation Prevents Poor Performance

Would you believe that many people don't bother to prepare for an interview because they just don't know what to prepare? They don't know what to expect in the way of questions, so they don't bother practicing or writing out examples. And, surprisingly, sometimes this works. But most of the time, "winging it" does not work. So, how can you prepare for this interview if you don't know what's going to happen when you get there? Let's begin by thinking about what an interview involves.

Just what is an interview, anyway? You could, more than likely, find a number of answers to this question. Using Wikipedia as a source, it seems the definition of an interview depends on how specific you get with your question.

Wikipedia defines an "interview" as: "a conversation between two or more people where questions are asked by the interviewer to elicit facts or statements from the interviewee." However,

Action-oriented (What will it take to demonstrate this factor?):

- Ability to handle stress in a fast-paced environment
- Ability to make things happen
- Ability to make quick decisions under pressure
- Ability to respond and adapt to situations under duress

Depending on the job you are seeking, you may be able to identify several more skills to show that you are action-oriented. The idea is to flush out what it will take to do the job. What does it mean when they say they want someone who is action-oriented? The more thoughts you can come up with, the more information you'll have to work with. These ideas will help you develop your answers with examples and stories.

Adaptability (What would it take to demonstrate that you are adaptable?):

- Flexible and open to new things
- Adjusts quickly to change
- Comfortable in new situations
- Willing to go above and beyond

Customer service (The job description will let you know who your customers will be.):

- Communication—relates well with others
- Able to handle difficult people and situations

- Patient and caring
- Able to make judgments and solve people problems

Integrity and trust (Most companies seek honest, trust-worthy employees.):

- Honest in all dealings
- Able to make difficult decisions when tested
- Can be trusted with confidential or company information
- Will do the right thing, even when no one is looking

Listening (Communication is more than being able to talk. Are you a listener?):

- Able to "hear" what others are saying and read between the lines
- Listens to problems and hears all the facts before making a decision
- Ability to make others feel as though they've been heard
- Listens more than talks in appropriate situations

This list of factors will determine the type of person that the interviewer is seeking. If you can demonstrate with your stories and examples that you are good with people and have great listening skills, it will go far toward proving your ability to handle customers, as listening is a big part of customer service. You should also think about times when your judgment affected your integrity and whether this is an area that you are following sections of this book, "honesty and integrity" would be high on your list as important factors the interviewer will be asking about.

See if you can flush out the rest of the factors using your job description.

- Skill needed?
  Key factors:

- Skill needed?
  Key factors:

- Skill needed?
  Key factors:

- Skill needed?
  Key factors:

- Skill needed?
  Key factors:

Repeat this exercise until you have several skills and key factors. Once you have identified the factors, this list will serve as the basis of your preparation for answering questions about these key factors.

This exercise will continue in Chapter 2, when we focus on what you have to offer. By placing the factors you identify on one side of a sheet, and what you have to offer on the other side, you will be able to see where you are a perfect match as well as the areas where you may fall short.

EXERCISE
Find the Factors, WITHOUT a Job Description or Posting

When you are lacking a job description, identifying the key factors will take some reading between the lines on your part. By following these steps, you will be able to piece together the key factors based on a consensus of job postings. Try your hand at this new technique.

- First, go to your favorite job search engine or any search site that posts job openings. You are going to search for a job description that you would like to apply for. At this point, don't be concerned about location or qualifications; you are doing an exercise. Remember, you are not going to apply to these job postings. You are using the postings for the words and content.
- Next, find postings of interest to you. Look for postings that are descriptive or that list key factors or core competencies.
- You will then print the postings out, maybe six or seven of them, depending on how descriptive the postings are.
- Next, take a highlighter or colored pen and mark the words that are similar in each posting. They don't have to be exactly the same, just in the same category. A word like "adaptable" could also be "flexible," or "willingness to go above and beyond."

Example: marketing manager

Job description: Marketing managers are responsible for the gross profit in assigned markets, and will own inventory, cost, pricing, and merchandising decisions for that market.

Responsibilities:

1. Develop and maintain supplier relationships at the property and chain level through daily contact.
   Key factors: communication skills; interpersonal sensitivity; create a motivational environment; informing

2. Analyze contracts and execute pricing.
   Key factors: strategic decision making; big picture perspective; negotiation

3. Implement Extranet rate and inventory revisions, ensure suppliers understand Extranet, and increase supplier usage of Extranet.
   Key factors: flexibility; informing; customer focus; motivate; accountable

4. Conduct weekly competitive analysis for key markets, report findings, and make adjustments.
   Key factors: analytical thinking; big picture thinking; development orientation; adaptable

5. Monitor, evaluate, and report on individual accounts and markets' progress toward achieving weekly, monthly, and annual targets.

Key factors: hold people accountable; analytical; decision maker, goal-oriented, big picture perspective

6. Understand key market hard/soft periods, know destinations and trends, create and maintain event calendars for key market locations, and plan courses of action required to meet supply, demand, and necessary sales.

   Key factors: business savvy; visionary; trend knowledge; organized; planner; implement action

7. Execute annual contract negotiations.

   Key factors: leadership; strategic; communication; deal-maker; closer; negotiation skill

Suggested key factors for this management position:

1. Communication: build relationships

2. Leadership: accountability to self and others

3. Analytical thinking: analysis of data

4. Visionary: big picture thinking

5. Ability to influence: motivate, sell, negotiate

6. Business savvy: understands and uses current business trends

Once you have read through any job description or posting you can select the key factors, regardless of the level of the job. It is important to be on the same page as the interviewer regarding the responsibilities of the job and what skills and traits it would take to successfully perform the job.

Sample Quiz: Reading Between the Lines

It's not about the questions, but the concerns behind the questions. Behind every interview question, there is a concern or another question. Your job is to process the question, thinking about what the interviewer's concern might be. In other words, why is the interviewer asking you this question? Can you identify the factors the interviewer is seeking?

Question: What kinds of people do you have difficulties working with?

(Interviewer's concerns: Team player? Able to adapt to new situations? Troublemaker?)

(Factor: ability to communicate and relate with others; adaptability to work in a diverse environment)

Question: When have you been most satisfied in your career?

(Interviewer's concern: What motivates you? Or demotivates you? Do you get bored easily?)

(Factor: motivation; job satisfaction; adaptable)

Question: How do you keep current and informed about your job and the industries that you have worked in?

(Interviewer's concern: Once you get the job do you continue to learn and grow? Do you stay challenged and motivated?)

(Factor: motivation; keeping abreast of current events; continued education or classes)

In Chapter 9 of this book, there is a final quiz to help you evaluate how well you can identify key factors after reading this book.

CHAPTER 2

Can This Candidate Do the Job?

What Do You Have to Offer?

For many people the most challenging part of a job interview is being able to "brag"—to let the interviewer know what they have accomplished in the past. This is unfortunate because unless the interviewer gets to know you and what you are capable of doing, he or she won't be able to know whether you are the right person for the job.

There needs to be a change in thinking here. First of all, talking about yourself in a job interview is not bragging; it's informing. Unfortunately, when you are unwilling to talk about your accomplishments, you are putting the burden on the interviewer to dig through your résumé to find this information. And, guess what? Interviewers either won't do that or, if they do, they won't like doing it. So, you are really making the interviewer's life a lot easier if you do the job of telling him or her about you and what you have to offer in this position. This chapter will focus on how you are qualified to do the job. The focus of this section will be about your knowledge-based skills; your transferable skills; and your personal traits and how to determine if you are a good match for the job.

By dividing your skills inventory into three categories, you will be able to assess and organize your presentation.

The Three Categories: Skills, Abilities, and Personal Traits

The three categories of skills, abilities, and traits are important in your preparation of differentiating yourself from the other candidates. When you look beyond the skills you have acquired through education and experience, you will see that you have other qualities and traits that make you a stronger contender to go up against other candidates, but more about those qualities and traits will be discussed in the following sections.

The Three Categories: Skills, Traits, and Abilities

1. *Knowledge-based skills* are skills learned through experience or education.

   Examples: computer programs/languages; graphics; writing skills; training skills; management experience; sciences: chemistry, biology; coaching skills, sales experience; leadership training; project management; operations; marketing; event planning; policy development; legal expertise; strategic planning; liaison; mediator; product management; research skills; business acumen; mechanically adept; and others.

2. *Transferable* or *general skills*: skills that can be thought of as "portable skills." You can take them with you to almost any job. They are broad-based and usually learned or acquired through experience.

    Examples: communication; listening; decision making; judgment; initiative; planning; organizing; time management; leadership; work ethic; interpersonal skills; common sense; social skills; creative ideas; sees big picture; analytical; accountable; reliable; high standards; resourceful; action-oriented; intuitive; problem solving; good with numbers; gets along well with others; articulate; handy; artistic; visionary.

3. *Personal traits*: qualities that make you unique. These traits can sometimes determine whether you are a good fit for the company, the department, or the position.

    Examples: dependable; strong; team player; versatile; patient; friendly; energetic; formal; loyal; self-confident; dynamic; practical; sociable; persuasive; responsible; sense of humor; cheerful; good attitude; aggressive; assertive; determined; honest; humble; productive; conscientious; curious; enthusiastic; precise; detail-oriented; compassionate; efficient; emotional; firm; open-minded.

The Knowledge-Based Skills: Education, Knowledge, and Experience

If you have submitted your résumé and have received a phone call, a phone screening, or an invitation to come for an in-person interview, the screeners have probably been impressed enough to find out more about you. The interviewer or screener wants to know if you can back up your résumé, or the statements or claims you have made on it, by providing examples and facts. It is likely that the interviewer(s) will ask questions to see if what you wrote—or had written by a professional résumé writer—can be verified as true statements. They will do this by asking questions to see if you are who you say you are. Can you really do the job? Have you embellished your résumé to the point where you aren't able to stand behind what you have claimed? What background experience can you tell about to substantiate what you've said? In other words, they will be looking at your examples of past behavior, successes and failures, as indicators of what you have done in the past. They are seeking your successes as examples of behavior that you can repeat— for them. If you did it before you can do it again.

The Job Description or Posting

It's now time to see if what you have to offer is a good match with the job descriptions for the jobs you are seeking. A job description usually starts with a list of "knowledge-based" requirements of the job. Here are some examples of knowledge-based requirements:

- Requires a B S degree in Health Sciences
- Bachelor's degree required, and an MBA preferred
- Minimum of two to four years of work-related experience is needed
- Approximately three to four years of relevant work experience desired
- At least five years of progressively responsible experience in project management
- Proficiency in PC applications, including Microsoft Word and Excel

Many of the requirements listed will be firmer, or less flexible, than others. It would be difficult to apply for a job that required computer program knowledge if you weren't familiar with computers or programs. But, if you take the time to read carefully, reading between the lines, you can see that there is some leeway for some of the requirements.

For example, the word "preferred" indicates that it would be great, but if you don't have the requirement you could still be considered. Of course, if you have the preferred skill you just moved closer to the desirable candidates list. The terms "preferred," desired," and "needed" may mean different things in companies. The word "approximately" leaves the door open to people with less or more years of experience. "At least five years of progressively ..." is a little more firm but still leaves some wiggle room when it comes to what constitutes the level of a "project." The word "proficiency" is open to interpretation because the definition of the word ranges from "expert" to "ability." If the description reads "or related area," this would widen the possibilities of you qualifying. When you read between the lines, you may feel more open to moving forward and taking a chance even though it might not be a perfect match.

Reading between the lines becomes more difficult when the job description uses words like "required," "must have," "certified," "licensed," "advanced degree," and "proven ability." There are some fields in which specific knowledge will be required, and you will not be able to work around these types of requirements. But there are as many jobs in which the requirements are softer than you may have thought previously.

Summarizing Your Knowledge-Based Education and Experience

This step will help you identify your knowledge-based skills, the skills you learned from experience and education.

Examples: analyzing; estimating; coordinating; negotiating; organizing; public speaking; mechanically adept; leadership; counseling; artistic; computer skills; entrepreneurial; design; budgeting; training; project management.

If you have a solid résumé, this part of the preparation should come directly from your résumé. A résumé often begins with a summary, which is useful to sum up what you have to offer. If you don't have a summary on your résumé, then you will have some organizing to do. But think of it as work that will help the interviewer understand your background. Some résumés are confusing because they do not follow a pattern. It is important that you can succinctly tell the interviewer about your education, years of experience, and the responsibilities you've had. The following work is preparation needed for the exercises in the following chapters, where we will organize the factors, skills, and abilities that make you unique.

EXERCISE

Your Knowledge-Based Skills

1. **Begin with your education.**

   What degrees do you have? Special training and certificate programs? Do you have any security clearances? Any certifications or licenses? Did you receive any special awards or commendations (particularly important for military candidates)?

2. **Next, years of experience.**

   Begin with your current position and the title or responsibility. Moving backward chronologically, go through your résumé. Many people want to start at the bottom and move up; this is a mistake. When you begin at the bottom and move up, by the time you get to your current position, the one that is probably of most interest to your interviewer, you have lost the interviewer's attention.

3. **What are your areas of expertise?**

   If the word *expert* concerns you, what do you know a great deal about? If you've worked in a job, you've acquired knowledge and experience. If you've taken classes, you've accumulated knowledge. By writing these facts, you will be preparing for exercises that will be covered in Part 4.

What Others Have Been Telling You

Some people have a real problem "blowing their own horn." If that is your problem, try using other people's words to boast about your accomplishments. When you use someone else's words to "brag" about you, it is called "third-party endorsement." In addition to being a great marketing tool, third-party endorsements are worth collecting because they provide a safe way of saying good things about yourself through others' words.

For example, if you say, "I did a great job on my project," it might sound like you're blowing your own horn, at least to you. But, if you say, "My boss was overwhelmed by the amount of money we were able to save using my idea, and he gave me a bonus to show his appreciation," it not only becomes a stronger and more powerful statement, but your boss is the one who made the statement. How great is that?

During the course of your education or work experience, perhaps you've received reviews or performance appraisals. These assessments are usually full of valuable information that you can share. Or, perhaps the feedback came through an informal remark or feedback from someone you worked with. However the information was conveyed, it is a valuable tool to use, especially if you are reluctant to say these things yourself.

Past Performance Comments

It will be worth your time and effort to prepare statements that tell the interviewer about your background and education.

Begin to think about yourself and what others have observed or experienced while working with you. What are the positive skills, abilities, and traits that you are known for? Maybe you've been told that you have an outstanding ability to build rapport with others. Or, you may have received an award or a commendation for doing something that was above and beyond what a job or situation required. It is very important to remember these events and comments so that you can write your examples and stories.

Interviewer's question: "If I were to ask your coworkers to tell me three positive things about you, what would they say?"

This may be an "OMG" question for you, but one that may be asked in one form or another in an interview. By writing a list of comments others have made about you, you may begin to see a pattern of skills and traits that others see in you. You will benefit from this preparation when you sit face-to-face with an interviewer. Interviewers are very interested in how you work and relate with others. What kind of a team player would you be? To give a good answer, begin to think back over your school and work history. Have you heard the same things said several times? Is there a pattern to the things that you've heard about yourself more than once?

Example

Factor: initiative

Your answer: "I improved a system and saved hundreds of man-hours as a result."

Answer with third-party endorsement: "My boss made a department announcement to acknowledge my significant contribution by coming up with a new system and gave me a gift card to a nice restaurant."

It is obvious that the third-party endorsement is much stronger and more memorable than your answer without the endorsement. The interviewer is now interested in hearing more about these significant accomplishments that impressed your boss so much. The endorsement does not always have to come from your boss. And, it does not have to be super significant. It's your accomplishment, whatever it was.

Was there a time when someone gave you credit or feedback about something you did? If you cannot come up with any, try reverting back to your reviews or performance appraisals, if you have them, and see if you can come up with some times when you were praised for something.

EXERCISE

Past Performance Comments

In the following exercise, try your hand at listing the factors that you have chosen, the accomplishments that relate to them, and what was said by whom.

Example:

Factor: (What factor are you going after?)
Accomplishment: (What was the result or outcome?)
Third-party endorsement: (By whom?)

Factor: (What factor are you going after?)
Accomplishment: (What was the result or outcome?)
Third-party endorsement: (By whom?)

Factor: (What factor are you going after?)
Accomplishment: (What was the result or outcome?)
Third-party endorsement: (By whom?)

Factor: (What factor are you going after?)
Accomplishment: (What was the result or outcome?)
Third-party endorsement: (By whom?)

Factor: (What factor are you going after?)
Accomplishment: (What was the result or outcome?)
Third-party endorsement: (By whom?)

Factor: (What factor are you going after?)
Accomplishment: (What was the result or outcome?)
Third-party endorsement: (By whom?)

This exercise is one that would benefit you to repeat until you have several third-party comments. Once you have identified these incidents, you will be able to use them to strengthen your comments in your stories about your past performance.

Knowledge-Based Skills Requirement

Knowledge-based skills may account for as much as 50 percent or more of the essential job function. Often these skills are the main focus of the job description, and some hiring decisions are made solely on the candidate's fulfillment of these requirements. While these decisions often turn out to be the wrong decisions because of the other traits that are essential to fitting into the culture or department of a company, it is something that you cannot control. Your job is to present yourself as qualified to do the job, and to tell the interviewer why you are the best person for the job.

Essential Skills: "Must Haves" for This Job

When reading through the job description, you should be aware of the language of the requirements. There will be some words that indicate that these are "critical skills" and are absolutely required in order to succeed in this particular job. Some examples:

- Experience using Internet protocols
- International experience
- Program development experience
- Special training required
- License needed
- Business acumen
- Very specific degree or experience such as law, technology, or engineering
- Security clearance
- U. S. citizenship required

If you fall short in these requirements, it will be unlikely that you will make it through the screening process. Perhaps you are looking in the wrong job category and need to rethink your goals. Try searching for other jobs in your field, or other fields in which some of the key factors and job requirements are a better match for you and what you have to offer. Simply sending out "blind" résumés to any job opening is not only a waste of time for you, but also frustrating when you don't get the response you want.

Your Knowledge-Based Skills

Starting with knowledge-based skills, what education, experience, special training, certificates, and licenses do you have that you want the employer to know about? You may be thinking, *They have all that information on my résumé.* The problem is that the interviewer may not have read your résumé. There is always the chance that he or she simply breezed through your résumé and now has only a vague picture of who you are and what you have to offer. A clue that the interviewer needs more information from you is when you are "asked": "Walk me through your résumé." In other words, "Read me your résumé and give me lots of details along the way because I haven't really read your résumé thoroughly."

When you begin to assemble information about your knowledge-based experience, it will be necessary to think about what to tell, and what will probably not be of interest to the interviewer for this particular job. For instance, the college where you received your degree may not be important. The details are more important to some positions than they are to others. Depending on the company, your degrees and where you earned them may be of major importance. And, some interviewers will be more impressed with big company experience such as Fortune 500 companies. Other companies will prefer experience in smaller settings, where you were able to be involved in a wider range of duties and responsibilities. It will be necessary for you to communicate your knowledge-based skills from your résumé, but to use judgment about how much detail to include. If this is a phone screening, this may be the only opportunity you will have to try for an invitation to an in-person interview, and you want to be sure the interviewer has a good picture of who you are and what you have to offer. Whenever you are interviewing, it is best to give the interviewer as much detailed information as possible about your background. Never assume anyone has the entire picture.

There are key skills that go hand in hand with knowledge-based skills. These are the skills you learned from experience and education.

Examples: analyzing; estimating; coordinating; negotiating; organizing; public speaking; mechanically adept; leadership; counseling; computer skills; entrepreneurial thinking; design; budgeting; training; project management.

Having the perfect match for the "knowledge-based" requirements area of the job may not be essential to your survival of the screening process, but the closer the match, the better your chances are of you hearing from the employer. When there is an influx of résumés and several well-qualified candidates for the employer to choose from, your chances thin out and this could be a problem. The words "could be" indicates that you may still have a chance if there is a good fit in other areas or you could bring added value to the position for one reason or another.

When all candidates appear equal in some of the essential requirements of knowledge and experience, it is sometimes an *added value* that will be the tiebreaker and determine which candidates to interview or even hire. Added-value skills or abilities are the skills and knowledge you have above and beyond what is essential for the job. These are skills, traits, or experiences that would be a plus in any position. An example would be a person with a foreign language skill that is pertinent to the job, perhaps a customer service job. Or, an ability to use sign language if you would be working with customers who would benefit from this service. These skills may not be essential to the job, but they may be something that you would bring to the job that would add value and be of interest to the employer.

Essential or Preferred?

Another significant reason to read the job description or posting several times is to carefully pick up on words that are ambiguous, such as "preferred." These are some examples of words on job descriptions that indicate there may be some leeway:

- Financial services industry experience *a plus*.
- Call center experience *preferred*.
- Excel and MS Project experience an *added value*.

- Passion for assisting disadvantaged persons would be a *great asset.*

- Second language skills and international business experience are *desired.*

The highlighted words indicate that it would be great, but not essential. Carefully reading the job description will provide you with information that indicates you are not only qualified, but you have added value to offer.

Examples of Knowledge-Based Statements

Below are examples of statements you can use to present your education and experience (beginning with your education).

I had a double major and earned a BA degree in economics and Spanish. I spent a semester in Spain living with a Spanish-speaking family and became quite fluent. For the past five years, I have been working in the mortgage industry, where I use my Spanish skills as needed.

I have recently completed my MBA and have been working in the finance area for four years. I also have an undergrad degree in business administration.

I have a BS in justice administration and am in the process of obtaining an MS in justice administration to be completed this fall. I have worked in sales for nine years, and also have a side business as a real estate investor.

I have a BA in accounting with a concentration in auditing. I also am studying to obtain my CPA license. I have worked for seven years in accounting, both in public and private accounting firms.

I have a BS in biology, cum laude. I completed an internship at a Fortune 500 company. I have worked in the biotech field for the past five years as a micro-biologist.

You will write your own statement in Chapter 5, "Tell Me About Yourself."

CHAPTER 3

Do We Like This Candidate? Will He or She Fit In?

t's a well-known fact that no two people are exactly the same; even twins, triplets, and other multiple birth siblings have differences. So, what makes you different from all the other candidates who are being interviewed? What do you have that makes you unique? What skills will break through any resistance to hire you as the right person for the job?

By thinking beyond the usual qualifications you have in the form of education and experience (knowledge-based skills), we will look at the other skills, traits, and abilities you have that will make you stand out from the others. The combination of all these skills makes you *unique*. You may have been taking some of these skills for granted, or be too modest to talk about them in an interview.

If knowledge-based skills account for as much as 50 percent or more of the essential job function, what accounts for the other 50 percent? The answer is your transferable skills and personal traits. This is the 50 percent of the job requirement that could give you a chance even if someone else has more knowledge-based skills than you do.

RULE OF THUMB

Leave your modesty at the door and bring your heart into the interview. Your heart is who you are—the real person.

Transferable Skills and Personal Traits

In this section, we will focus on transferable skills and personal traits, as these are the qualities that could make the difference between the hiring of one equally qualified candidate over another. This is the part of the interview that is more subjective. Unfortunately, this is where many candidates begin their spiral descent out the door.

Most job interviews last anywhere from an hour or less to an all-day or weekend event. For some positions, the interview can last all day and involves interactions with many individuals from the company. But on average, the majority of interviews last about an hour per session with an individual or a panel of interviewers. The interview schedule will really depend on the position you are applying for, its level of responsibility, as well as the company's culture and policies about the hiring process. The longer the interview, the more time the interviewer will have to evaluate your behavior and personality and really get to know you.

How can someone get to know you in one hour? The answer is they really can't. This is why the person who sells himself or herself best will be make the most memorable impression and will more than likely get the job offer. Your challenge is to be prepared to let the interviewer see who you are through your performance during the interview. This includes your ability to act and talk confidently about your past behavior, your accomplishments, and yourself.

The most important part of this category is to let the interviewer get to know the real you. When you hold back, the interviewer will not get a realistic picture of you and your personality. Try to remember that the interviewer is thinking, *Would I want to work with this person?*

People's personalities vary, and for some people the idea of "telling it all" at the first meeting feels very uncomfortable and dangerous. Others will tell too much and forget this is not a "date" or an opportunity to make a new best friend; it is a job interview. Do not underestimate your personality traits as a deal breaker when there are two or more very qualified candidates. The following is feedback received from a client:

Every time I was asked a question I thought of the factor; that was the key. I also remembered to emphasize my personality and be myself. There was another female candidate who was interviewing, so I had competition. She had more job experience than I had, and a lot more years in the industry, so I was intimidated and threatened. But, as we sat waiting she never exchanged a single word to anyone, not even a "Good morning." It was then that I realized I had something she didn't: my personality. One of the things that my teammates tell me all the time is they like working with me, and that they enjoy my sense of humor because it lightens the mood and relieves pressure. So, during the interview I was relaxed and used my personality and sense of humor. I had the interviewers smiling and laughing. I kept remembering what you told me: "Be yourself and talk to these people like they are your colleagues." I reminded myself that this wasn't an interrogation, and I relaxed and was myself.

The good news is I got the job! Even though the other female had more experience than I did, they decided that I was the one they wanted to work with. Being genuine made all the difference.

Letting the interviewer get to know you during an interview and using the key factors as identified can make a huge difference in showing and convincing the interviewer that you are the right person for the job. That is not to say that if you are a quiet, reserved person that you should go into the interview cracking jokes. It is very important to be yourself. If this isn't the right place for you, it's better to find out during the interview instead of two or three days, or even weeks into the job. Job fit goes both ways. The idea is to find a place that is the right place for you. A place where you can contribute and stay motivated about what it is you do, as well as what the company does.

EXERCISE

Identifying Your Transferable Skills

By taking an inventory of your transferable skills, you can determine some of the traits that you may have been neglecting to talk about in your interviews. This exercise is about identifying and writing about the skills that

---

some people refer to as your "soft skills." We will refer to them as transferable skills because they are portable, meaning that you can take them with you to any job or industry.

Examples: communication; planning; time management; problem solving; customer service; teaching; coaching; creative; researching; selling; follow-through; resourcefulness; attention to detail; skilled with numbers; innovative.

You may notice that many transferable skills are closely tied to the job factors we've covered earlier in the book. When you are reading a job description or posting, you will notice that once the job description moves beyond the qualifications of education and years of experience required, it begins to focus on the factors that are desired in a candidate. This is where you will recognize the value of your transferable skills.

Examples of words you would find on a job description are listed below, along with the transferable skills it would take to do the job:

- The job description: ability to communicate verbally; relate effectively with others
  (Your transferable skills and experiences: communication; ability to convince others; negotiation skills; conflict resolution experience)

- The job description: ability to organize, plan, and prioritize

(Your transferable skills and experiences: time management; attention to detail; follow-through; multitasking)

- The job description: ability to relate effectively with others
(Your transferable skills and experiences: communication; listening skills; problem solving; trust)
- The job description: ability to evaluate information and make judgments/decisions
(Your transferable skills and experiences: ability to analyze; problem solving; analytical thinking)
- The job description: initiative and motivation
(Your transferable skills and experiences: steps forward and takes action; willing to do above and beyond; can-do attitude; makes things happen)
- The job description: ability to adapt to changing situations
(Your transferable skills and experiences: flexible; willing; good attitude; fits in; risk taker)
- The job description: honesty and integrity
(Your transferable skills and experiences: ability to make difficult decisions; do the right thing; use good judgment; is trustworthy)

By focusing on the requirements of the job posting and then breaking it down to select your transferable skills, you may discover skills that you have been overlooking. These skills could make a difference in the way you sell yourself in a confident manner.

Identifying Personal Traits

Personal traits are the individual qualities that make you who you are. Are you outgoing, and do you tend to jump right in? Or, do you take time to warm up before you let someone get to know you? Do you always think ahead and meet deadlines before they are due? Or, are you a last minute person who gets that rush when working against the clock to meet a deadline? This is not about what's good or not good; it's about you and your character. Some jobs fit one type of personality but would be absolutely boring to another person. The idea is to find the right person for the right job so that everyone wins.

Here are some of the attributes that define a person's personality: dependable, strong, team player, versatile, patient, friendly, energetic, formal, loyal, self-confident, dynamic, practical, sociable, persuasive, responsible, sense of humor, cheerful, good attitude, aggressive, assertive, determined, honest, humble, productive, conscientious, curious, enthusiastic, precise, detail oriented, compassionate, efficient, emotional, rigid, open-minded, and so on.

Question: How Would You Describe Your Personality?

This is a straightforward question, but if you answer too hastily you may end up sounding like every other candidate. What makes you unique?

Interviewers ask this question for a couple of reasons: to hear where you place the emphasis in your description, and to see how quickly and creatively you can think on the spot. Remember, the interviewer is trying to judge whether you will fit in.

Spice Up Your Answer

Don't give the interviewer the same tired, old answers everybody else gives. Try thinking of new ways to get your message across and sound enthusiastic about your personal traits. The following are some examples of boring answers and then better ones to describe your personality.

Boring answer: "I am a high energy person."
This answer needs more detail and energy.
Better answer: "I am a person who is energized by challenges and problems."

Boring answer: "I'm a hard worker."
This is the most common phrase used when answering the question about strengths. It shows no imagination.
Better answer: "I do whatever it takes to get the job done, sometimes working 10-hour days."

Boring answer: "I am a quick learner."
This is a very overused phrase that has lost its effectiveness.
Better answer: "I can hit the ground running and come up to speed faster than anyone I know."

Boring answer: "I'm analytical."
This is a lackluster answer that doesn't reveal much information.
Better answer: "I'm known for my ability to analyze data and transform it into useful information."

Boring answer: "I'm very organized."
This is a very understated answer.
Better answer: "I am a person who knows how to bring order to chaos."

Boring answer: "I'm reliable."

This answer needs more information to get the point across.

Better answer: "I pride myself on my record of never missing deadlines, regardless of what it takes."

Boring answer: "I'm good with customers."

The answer needs clarification—good in what way?

Better answer: "I know how to build great relationships with customers. They always ask for me personally."

EXERCISE

Scripting Your Personal Traits

Describing your personality is somewhat like writing an advertisement for a product. In this case however, the product is YOU.

Think about why a customer would choose you as opposed to another product. What makes you unique? Are you the type of person who would fit into this organization? Your job is to convince your interviewer that you are the person for the job by going beyond your knowledge-based and transferable skills to include some of your personal traits.

Try your hand at making a list of personality traits that describe you. These are the qualities you would like the interviewer to remember after the interview. See if you can spice up your answers to show that you are a good personality match.

Requirement: "Must have five or more years of experience managing a diverse population of employees."

Boring answer: "I work well with all types of people."

This is a rather flat statement and not specific. Try a new slant using more powerful words.

Your answer: ?

Try this exercise by going through a job description or posting line by line and picking out a possible question an interviewer might ask. Once you've completed that part of the exercise, begin to answer the questions with interesting answers.

Better answer: "I am a person who values others' qualities and contributions. My team members would tell you that I am a very fair manager who listens when they have something to say." (Notice the third-party endorsement.)

The more specific your answers, the better your chances are of leaving a lasting impression. Interviewers talk to several candidates in a single day. What will make you a memorable candidate?

In today's competitive job market, it is important to take some time to think about how you could describe your personality in a way that will make you stand out. The buyer needs to be sold on your uniqueness and abilities. When you sound like everybody else, you look like everybody else. Distinguishing yourself from the pack will give you an edge. A little work before the interview will put some zip into your pitch.

Reading the Job Posting One Line at a Time: What Are They Looking for?

Sample job posting:

> We are looking to hire 10 additional account managers and customer service positions.

> Job requirements:
> - College degree (knowledge-based)
> - Sales and/or marketing experience a plus, but not a requirement (knowledge-based)
> - Integrity (transferable skill or personal trait)
> - Exemplary ambition for success (personal trait)
> - Competitive and proactive attitude (personal trait)
> - Confident demeanor (personal trait)
> - Strong student mentality (transferable skill)

EXERCISE
Is There a Match?

As with previous exercises in this book, you will need a job posting or job description. This time you will read the description with the idea of selecting the job requirements that require transferable skills or personal traits, rather than education and experience.

Using a piece of paper or a Word document, write "What they are looking for," on one side, and "What I have to offer" on the other side. Each time you apply for a position, it will be invaluable to do this exercise so that you will know how close a match you are to the requirements of the job.

Example

The Job Posting (Needs) and My Qualifications

Education and Experience

Marketing experience

- Five-plus years as a marketing consultant
- Significant consumer marketing in retail

Product management experience

- Led product marketing efforts for online store
- Spearheaded product management effort for major retail chain as product manager

Transferable Skills

Analytical abilities

- Excellent qualitative and quantitative marketing analysis; high impact results

Plan and organize

- Planned and organized company events for trade shows and recruiting events
- Multitasked several key projects successfully, resulting in increased revenue

Evaluate/make judgments

- Analyzed cost factors and decided on price increase on key products; resulted in 25% increase

Initiative and motivation

- Motivated team by setting up contests, resulting in increased sales and team spirit
- Developed technique to save on shipping costs and increase revenue per product

Communication ability
- Leadership qualities: ability to lead projects and teams to successful outcomes
- Ability to communicate to all levels of management; ability to influence others

Interpersonal Skills

Adaptable
- Worked in multiple locations, interfaced with a wide diversity of people at all levels
- Worked various shifts in last job as needed
- On-call 24/7
- Learned new programs in record time; assisted others as needed

Highly competitive
- Team captain of rugby team; team won first place three years in a row
- Graduated in top 10 percent of class in training group.
- Met and exceeded all sales goals in quarter

You may notice that sometimes there is an overlap between transferable skills and personal traits. A good example of an overlap between skills and traits is the communication requirement:

Communication skills: ability to lead projects and teams to successful outcomes; ability to communicate to all levels of management; ability to influence others.

While these skills all fit under communication skills, there is an overlap here that requires relating to others.

What does it take to have good communication skills? You may have answered or thought "talking to others." That's a correct answer, but communication is far more than talking in most jobs.

For example, it may mean being able to handle yourself in stressful situations like a customer service position; or it could mean your ability to convince others to change things your way in a sales or negotiation situation. This is where you begin to read between the lines.

If you are going to apply for a sales position, the communication skills required will be quite different than if you are applying for a scientific position. The salesperson will need good customer service with an ability to convince others that his or her way is the best way. The scientist will require good communication skills to be able to write his findings in an understandable report or to present findings to fellow colleagues or members of the community. Two different methods of relaying information, but both examples fall under the factor "communication," and will also require a different emphasis on relating to people. Both are transferable skills and personal traits.

Once you've completed this exercise, you will be more prepared to start thinking about your examples and stories to include in all three categories of skills and traits. This becomes a key building block for other exercises in your preparation that we will discuss in the following parts of the book.

Is This a Good Place for You?

This process can also be used as a tool for you to judge whether this is the job you thought it was. Would this job be a good fit for you and your personality? Are you an "action-oriented" person? Have you demonstrated an ability to stay cool under pressure or adapt to stressful situations? If you have, this is good. If you have done this in the past and never want to work that way again, this is not so good.

These factors are clues for what the interviewer is seeking in a candidate, but it also works as a check and balance system to find out if this is the job for you. Do you want pressure and stress in a job? Does that fit your personality? Or, should you pass on this job even though you are qualified? The answers to these questions will be determined by your needs, your situation, and your values.

CHAPTER 4

Can We Afford This Candidate?

This section will cover the basics of dealing with questions and rules of salary negotiation. Since salary negotiation is not the focus of this book, we will not go into the details or the complex issues involved in negotiations as some other books are dedicated to the subject. This chapter will deal with the questions that are the most common in the interview process. We are mainly focusing on what the interviewer is seeking when asking questions regarding salary.

Most companies have preset salary ranges determined by participating in salary surveys. They are averaged with other companies to establish "the going rate." Job descriptions and salaries are compared, and the averages are calculated and shared by the participants of these surveys. The ranges tend to be wide, and all have a high, a median, and a low. The majority of companies typically start salaries somewhere in the area of the middle or median of the range. This is important to know because people tend to look at the high end of the range when they do research about the "going rate" and expect to receive that salary, without taking into consideration that there is a low end of the range.

There are many reasons the interviewer wants to know your specific salary requirement. He or she mainly wants to see if your required salary fits within the range budgeted. Reading between the lines, the interviewer's question is, "Can we afford this candidate?"

If you are asked what salary you are expecting, this could be a strategic moment when your chances of moving to the next stage of the interview process are at stake. When asked for salary requirements you could price yourself right out of the running before you even get a chance to sell yourself.

If your salary requirement is too high, this could be a reason to terminate the screening or interviewing process: "We can't afford this person; he is looking for a salary out of our acceptable range."

If your salary requirement is too low, this could be a reason to suspect that you are not at the level of expertise they are looking for: "This person is too far below the range to have had the experience we need."

You can see this is a lose/lose situation for everyone involved if the question is asked prematurely and you answer the question flat out.

Here are examples of salary questions interviewers ask:

"What salary are you seeking?"

"What salary are you making at your current job?"

"What salary were you making at your last job?"

Examples of premature answers:

> "I was making $50,000."
>
> "I am currently making $50,000 a year with a yearly bonus."
>
> "I am looking for a 15 percent increase over what I am currently making."

This is too much information too soon. It is in your best interest to postpone giving an exact number if possible. You need more information about the job and the salary structure of the company including benefits, bonuses, salary reviews, and the company's philosophy of paying at a certain level.

How Much Are You Worth?

A fundamental rule for buying anything is to first learn what it is worth and what the going rate is for this object. If you were going to buy a car, a house, or make any major purchase, you would first check to see what the average price is for the item. Knowing the price of something is a basic principle, and it's the same principle that applies to job interview preparation. Before you begin your job search, there is some information that you will need to research:

- What are you worth?
- What is the going rate in your geographical location, in your field, for your particular job title?
- What is your education and years of experience worth?

There is no longer any excuse for your being caught off guard if you have access to a computer. The Internet provides all the information you need. In addition to the Internet you can do this research by checking with colleagues (if they will talk about their salary; this is a guarded secret for most people). One way to get around resistance is to talk about "ranges." You can also contact associations in your industry as they often have salary survey information. And, the U.S. government also provides salary information.

Before you can even think about applying for a job, you should be thinking about salary issues. It is in your best interest to do research to locate information about your worth. The Appendix at the back of this book will provide resources regarding salary sites to research.

The Salary Question Process

The salary process is delicate, and once it begins it's almost like a dance between the interviewer and the candidate: one step forward, one step back, step together, and back again. To perform the steps you must have a good sense of your value and worth. The employer takes the lead and you follow. You move together through the process, aware of the other, taking care not to step on one another. The process is never confrontational or harsh, but smooth and in harmony.

Phone Screening Can Catch You Off Guard

It is not uncommon for the first step of the interview process to begin on the phone as a screening process. The interviewer may catch you off guard by calling at some unexpected time and immediately ask for your salary requirement or what salary you are currently making. Even though you may feel a bit tongue tied, be careful to consider your options before you answer. If you are too low or too high, this could end the interview. It is best to delay giving a direct answer until you have no choice.

Examples:

Interviewer's question: "Could you tell me your salary requirement?"

Candidate's answer: "I'd be glad to talk salary at the appropriate time, but I really don't have enough facts at this time to discuss salary. I would be interested in hearing the range budgeted for this position as well as the entire benefits package."

Or, you could say:

Candidate's answer: "What does your company typically pay someone with my background and experience?"

Postponing the salary discussion is the best step for you, at least until you have the information you need. If the interviewer pushes for a "ballpark" or "what you are making now," you could talk about ranges as in the following example.

Candidate's answer: "I've done some research and have found an acceptable range for someone with my years of experience and education is (name a range). Is this the range that your company has budgeted for the position?"

By realizing what is behind the question and being prepared to talk about salary on your terms, you will change your position and not feel like your back is up against the wall. You will be able to talk "ranges and going rates," and not fear revealing your hand or losing out on a "better offer."

But, what if the representative is having none of your vague answers and pushes you for your "current" or "last salary?" Here are some possible answers, keeping in mind what's behind this question.

Candidate's answer: "I'm just not ready to talk salary without some more information from the company and what the job will entail so that I have something to compare it with. Rather than go back and forth, the range I would be interested in is $ [name a starting figure] to $ [name a closing figure]." Be sure the range is broad with an acceptable number at the low end. If you are offered your low-end number, you were the one who named the number, and it may be the number that they consider acceptable for you.

Or, you could say something like:

Candidate's answer: "The base salary that I received in my last job was combined with an extremely generous benefits package and bonuses. I would need to hear the details of the package that you offer in order to compare." (If, of course, this is true)

Everything Has a Price Tag

When you consider any information about salary, you must remember to take into account the "full package." Every benefit and bonus adds on dollars to your salary number.

Example: At your last company, you received three weeks of paid vacation, plus personal time off. How much does three weeks of vacation cost the company? That is a paid benefit.

At this company they have three weeks of vacation, but that includes your personal time off. You just lost some days off. What is the value lost? Or, perhaps this company only offers two weeks of paid vacation. What have you lost in the way of benefit compensation?

Negotiating Is Not for Everyone

Have you ever negotiated an offer? If not, you are not alone. Most people do not negotiate salary. They accept what is offered.

The Package Story

This is an example of someone who jumped at an offer before doing his homework:

Nicholas received an on-the-spot offer and was thrilled. This was the job he wanted, and he was anxious to get started. He was going to get more money and a bonus. What more could he ask for? He accepted on the spot.

When he got home that evening, he sat down with pencil and paper and began to evaluate the offer and what he was getting overall. He was not only shocked by what he discovered, but wished that he could go back and talk about some of the issues. But he had signed on the "dotted line" that afternoon.

Once you sign the offer letter, you have essentially signed a contract. It is too late to go back and negotiate. Try not to accept an on-the-spot offer unless it is absolutely out of this world or you are desperate and don't want the offer to go away. It is generally wise to evaluate what you are gaining and losing. Let's look at what Nicholas found out by doing some simple calculations.

Nicholas was offered $55,000 per year, with a hiring bonus of $5,000 paid in two payments over the next six months. This was a $5,000 increase from what he was making on his last job and a bonus to boot: an extra $10,000.00.

When he and his wife looked over the benefits package, however, they discovered that he would now have to pay the insurance premiums for his dependents. His last employer had paid the premiums for the entire family.

This would cost him $350.00 per month, or $4,200 per year.

His new vacation package gave him two weeks time off, accrued over the next 12 months. His former package included three weeks vacation.

This decreased his compensation by $962.00, one week's vacation pay.

Nicholas was receiving a 6.5 percent yearly bonus based on company earnings in his last position. His new company does not have a planned bonus as part of the salary. Bonuses are earned based on performance, and given as judged appropriate.

This was a decrease of $3,250.00 per year, the lost bonus.

His former employer matched 50 cents for every dollar contributed up to 6 percent on his 401(k) account. This company does not match funds.

This was a decrease of $1,500.00 per year (based on 6 percent contribution).

His calculations showed a minus of almost $10,000 a year from his new offer, based on cost of insurance premiums, lost bonus, and lost matching 401(k) contributions. He wasn't quite so thrilled with the offer anymore.

At least he got that $5,000 hiring bonus, which will cushion the fall. But even that will be affected, as he didn't anticipate the higher tax rate on "special" checks that was deducted from the bonus money. These higher rate taxes can run as high as 41.5 percent.

Nicholas got the job he wanted, and maybe that is worth more to him than the money difference. But it would have been wiser to make the decision with all the facts before signing the offer letter. He might have been able to negotiate another $5,000 to compensate for the difference in benefits. Or, given the higher tax rate, he could have negotiated for an increase in the hiring bonus.

It is best to take some time to reflect on the "total package." Benefits can be worth another 20 percent to 50 percent of your salary. There are other factors to consider besides money: more challenging work, a better company, or a greater opportunity. It may be worth giving up dollars now to invest in your future. However, the decision should be thought through before rushing ahead.

One more issue to take into account is when you are going to start your new job; it is a good idea to find out when yearly reviews and increases take place. Not all companies have annual reviews and raises, but if this one does, it is something to factor into your calculations before accepting an offer at certain times of the year.

If pressed to give your answer to an offer on the spot, always stall for time. Tell them that you need to do some calculations and think about it. There is only one window of opportunity to negotiate your terms of employment. Once you say yes, the window closes.

Of course, if you have been out of work for some time, the salary discussion may change because your salary history may not be current. In fact, you may be satisfied with an offer that is the "going rate." This is a very individual issue based on your situation and your needs.

Your Salary Needs

Before the interview, it is a good idea to do an inventory of your basic financial needs beginning with your *fixed monthly total*. These are the fixed costs that must be paid every month, no matter what is happening. They include your cost for living accommodations, utilities, telephone, credit cards, insurance, Internet provider, car payment, and similar expenses.

Next there are the *variable fixed expenses*. These expenses include the personal spending you do on clothes, food, grooming, entertainment, education, travel, and so on.

Together, these numbers make up your *total living expenses*. These numbers in turn will serve as a guide to what you need to earn to survive and whether you can afford to take an offer. It is important that you know these numbers to help decide what to accept. If the offer that is being made is $1,000 a month short of your total living expenses, you will have to assess where or if you can cut back. You may have to turn down an offer because it will not support your total cost of living.

These are very personal decisions that will affect your willingness to interview for this job if the salary is not what you need. Your needs will determine the discussion and steps you take.

The Face-To-Face Interview

The subject of your current salary or your salary requirement will not be limited to the "phone screen" alone. These types of questions will more than likely come up again during the in-person interview. It is in your best interest to let the interviewer bring up the subject of money first. You will be busy letting the interviewer know why you are the best candidate for the job and why you are worth more than the "going rate."

The Basic Principles of Salary Negotiation

Keep the following in mind throughout:

1. You can't negotiate anything until you have an offer. Don't go there yet.

2. Know your walk-away point—when you can't afford to take the offer.

3. Know the rules of salary negotiation before discussing salary. (See below.)

4. Know what you want: the whole package and the priorities of wants.

Applying the Principles

The examples below are situations that demonstrate the need to be familiar with the basic principles of salary negotiation before you begin your interviewing process. Being knowledgeable about some basic rules can make the difference between success and increased dollars, or failure or even accepting an offer that doesn't "feel" good.

What Would You Do?

You go to the interview prepared with the numbers you need and what you want in the way of salary. When the interviewer asks you questions about salary, you are prepared and ready with answers.

When asked what your salary requirements are, you have several options:

- You can tell the interviewer what you were making at your last job. (Not recommended if you can avoid giving this number out.)

- You can give a range that is acceptable to you, making sure that the lowest number is enough to cover your basic needs. (This is the best way of handling this difficult question.)

- You can ask for a range that this position typically pays. (Getting the interviewer to name the number first is the best position for you.)

- You can postpone the discussion until you have more facts about the company and the entire package. (If possible, this is the best scenario for you.)

There is no right or wrong answer, but how you handle this discussion will be key to your ability to try to negotiate a higher offer or package.

The Offer

If the employer determines that you are right for the job, the company will take the lead and make an offer. It is now your turn to move the dance to the next stage. But first, you must evaluate the package. Take into consideration the:

- Base rate (always the top priority) and timing of annual reviews
- Alternative compensation: bonus, commission, stock options, profit sharing
- Benefits: premiums for insurance, paid time off, matching 401(k), working conditions
- Other perks: car, education reimbursement, training, laptop computer

Some basic calculations will tell you how closely the offer meets your needs, values, and worth.

The Seven Rules of Salary Negotiation

Rule One: He who mentions a dollar figure first, loses.
Rule Two: Never try to negotiate until you have an offer.
Rule Three: Do not accept on-the-spot offers.
Rule Four: Always get the offer in writing.
Rule Five: Keep it friendly.
Rule Six: Consider your position before making deals.
Rule Seven: Focus on the base first.

The Seven Rules of Salary Negotiation

This section explains in more detail how to apply the seven rules of salary negotiation.

Rule One: He Who Mentions a Dollar Figure First, Loses

Wait until the subject is broached. Then answer that you are open on salary and are looking for an opportunity or that you would like to postpone that discussion until later in the process. This is a good time to ask what salary range is budgeted for the position. If you are asked what your former salary was, you might state that you would like to hear more about the responsibilities of the job before you compare salaries, or that there were circumstances in your other job that kept your salary below market value. If you are asked what salary you are looking for, depending on where you are in the interviewing process, state that you think it is too early to discuss salary and you would like to hear more about the job before you discuss the particulars of money.

Rule Two: Never Try to Negotiate Until You Have an Offer

You are in a far stronger position to negotiate after you have the offer. Your chances of getting a higher salary improve if the interviewer is convinced you are the right person for the job. This falls somewhere between "They want you" (they're ready to make an offer) and "They got you!" (you've signed on the dotted line, and it is too late to go back and start over).

RULE OF THUMB

Never try to negotiate anything until there's an offer.

Rule Three: Do Not Accept On-the-Spot Offers

Some employers make on-the-spot offers. It is always a good idea to take time to think the offer over. Once you've accepted the offer, it's too late to negotiate any terms of the agreement. If pressed for a decision, tell the employer that you have a personal policy of taking 24 hours to think over major decisions.

Rule Four: Always Get the Offer in Writing

Too many people have been burned after negotiating a sweet deal only to find that when management changes, there is no record of the negotiation. Get it in writing! If you negotiate a change, make sure you get a new offer letter or an addendum memo. An e-mail is acceptable as a formal document.

Rule Five: Keep It Friendly

The tone of the negotiation should never be confrontational. You should be aiming for a win/win situation.

Rule Six: Consider Your Position Before Making Deals

If you cannot settle on a salary, perhaps an early performance review/salary increase can be negotiated. Sometimes you can negotiate using vacation or benefits. The answer is always no unless you ask the question.

Rule Seven: Focus on the Base First

It is in your best interest to negotiate the base salary first. Your future raises will be affected by this sum, not to mention Social Security, unemployment, life insurance, and others.

Sometimes the employer's hands are tied due to internal salary equity. You may be asking for more money than some of the current employees are making. Sometimes you will be offered a hiring bonus.

CHAPTER 5

Tell Me About Yourself

The ultimate question in any encounter with someone you don't know is, "Who are you, anyway?" When one person is getting to know another person, the most common request is "Tell me about yourself." Those may not be the exact words used, but the question will be there:

"What do you do?"

"What's your background?"

"Where are you from?"

"What do you like to do?"

"Where do you work?"

How this question is answered will depend on the situation and the setting. But the same challenge will always be there:

"What do I say?"

"How much information should I give?"

"I don't know where to start or where to focus."

Not surprising, one of the most frequent ways to begin a job interview is the interviewer asking something like "Why don't we begin by you telling me something about yourself?"

On the surface this appears to be a straightforward question, but if you answer too hastily you may end up sounding like every other candidate. The answer you give to this question will set the tone for the rest of the interview. For some candidates, this is the most challenging question in the interview to answer. Why? Because of the unknowns and the trust issues involved. You may be thinking, "I don't know this person, why should I tell her everything there is to know about me?" The answer is because if you don't tell her about yourself, she won't get to know you. And who is going to hire someone he or she didn't get to know? This is a key issue in interviewing: how do you connect with the interviewer in such a short period of time?

For the more extroverted person, answering this question may not be as big a challenge as it is for the more introverted person, who thinks answering this question is pure torture. If you are the type of person who needs time to warm up to a stranger and establish trust before you start talking about yourself, you will want to work on some before-the-interview preparation to feel more in control about what you are going to say.

If you are a more extroverted person, you will need to draw some boundaries about how much you are going to tell the interviewer. An analogy I use with clients is:

"Open your shirt one button at a time. You don't have to show everything right away."

In fact, if the interviewer is a more introverted type of person, and you are a highly extroverted person, you may be coming off as a "tsunami": too much information given too soon.

Preparing ahead of time and using the company's job description to identify what the interviewer is seeking in a new hire will help you craft a statement that can make you stand out from the competition.

A Tragic Example: "Tell Me About Yourself"

Eleanor dreaded this question, and when it was the first one asked at her interview, she fumbled her way through with a vague answer, not focusing on what she would bring to the job.

> *I'm happily married, and originally from Denver. My husband was transferred here three months ago, and I've been getting us settled in our new home. I'm now ready to go back to work. I've worked in a variety of jobs, usually customer service related. I'm looking for a company that offers growth opportunities.*

The interview went downhill after that. Her first mistake was starting with personal information (illegal for the interviewer to ask in an interview, but in this case she volunteered the information: "I am married") and giving the interviewer reason to doubt whether she was an employee who would stay for very long. Looking at this scenario from the interviewer's perspective, you can see why Eleanor did not get a second interview or an offer.

- **Interviewer's concern:** She's married, and when her husband gets transferred that means she has to leave. She did it before and she can do it again.

- **Interviewer's concern:** She has some work experience with customers, but she didn't emphasize what she did. Will she be able to do this job?

- **Interviewer's concern:** She is looking to "grow." Although I like a person who is interested in "growing," what about the job she is applying for? Will she stay content for long? I'm looking to fill this job right now.

Coaching Eleanor to Success

How could Eleanor have approached this differently? If Eleanor had a job description, the first thing she could have done was to read through it and find out what it would take to do this job.

One of the first things that Eleanor needed to do was to begin thinking about her strengths and how they matched the job posting she was preparing to interview for.

The Job Posting
Eleanor's Experience

Three to five years of customer service experience

- Worked in a variety of settings, working with customers for over five years.

Must be able to work with difficult people

- She is strong in communications and at connecting with people.
- She has a strong background and proven success with customer relationships.

Organization and follow-through are a must

- Her key strength is her follow-through.
- She prides herself on her reputation for meeting deadlines.

Eleanor had many factors that the employer was seeking in an employee, but she had diluted her answer by talking about her marriage and setting up the house. This information is not only unnecessary information that is not of interest to the interviewer, but it hurt her chances of getting the job by focusing on the wrong things.

She could have selected the key factors the employer was looking for and prepared her stories and answers based on those factors. By reading between the lines, she would have seen that some of her transferable skills and personal traits made up for her being out of the work force for a while.

The next thing Eleanor could have done was to know her strengths and what she had to offer, not only in knowledge-based skills, but her broad experience working with customers and her ability to build relationships. By doing some simple exercises, she could have been prepared to let the interviewer know that she was worth the risk of hiring someone who might not stay long term because she had the skills and traits the company was seeking in an employee.

Eleanor, Take Two

Eleanor is prepared to answer the question, "Tell me about yourself" this time:

> *I am a person who thrives on solving problems, particularly "people problems." For the past five years I have worked in a wide variety of settings—everything from retail to manufacturing—and I never met a problem I couldn't work through.*
>
> *I have very strong communication skills and know how to make connections with people. Anyone who has worked with me would tell you that I am highly organized and known for my follow-through and attention to detail.*

This time, Eleanor not only was given a second interview, but she was given a job offer. She had intrigued the interviewer from the start when she emphasized her ability to work with any type of person in a variety of settings, plus her strong communication skills and organizational ability. That was exactly what the interviewer was seeking in a candidate. After all, that's what it said in the job posting.

Walk Me Through Your Résumé

When an interviewer starts the interview with the request "Walk me through your résumé," she is asking a different question than "Tell me about yourself." This is true in reverse: when an interviewer asks the "tell me about" question, he or she is not wanting to hear you walk through your résumé.

The next mistake people make is that they start talking from the bottom of the résumé to answer this question, and then work forward to the present. By the time you get to your current position, the interviewer has more than likely lost interest or is taking a snooze. Hopefully, you have written your résumé with the most current experience at the top and then worked backward. So, why would you start at the bottom and move forward to answer a question about your experience?

When the interviewer asks you to "Walk me through your résumé," there's a good chance that he or she hasn't spent much time studying your résumé. Sometimes a résumé reader will scan the résumé for certain information and then rely on you to summarize the rest of the résumé for him or her. If this happens to you, be ready to hit the "high spots" so that the interviewer can get a good picture of who you are.

Focus, Script, and Practice

The secret to success with a free-form question like: "Tell me about yourself," is to focus, script, and practice. You cannot afford to "wing" this statement, as it will have an effect on the rest of the interview. Begin to think about what the interviewer is seeking in a candidate and what you have that matches the experience, skills, and traits required.

EXERCISE

Your Qualifications, Their Requirements

Begin with the job posting or description and list the strengths that you have pertinent to the job's requirements (experiences, skills, and traits).

My Qualifications

What are they seeking in a candidate?

Requirements, must haves?

Desired, would be a plus?

What factors are required?

What transferable skills do I have that match the factors?

What personality traits are they seeking to do the job?

Are you beginning to see the importance of the job posting or description, the key factors, the three categories of concerns, and the need to do your homework before going on your next interview?

While it's important to prepare this information, it does not mean you should "memorize" information. In fact, *do not memorize anything.* When you memorize you tend to sound like a robot and not like yourself. Remember, your goal is to let the interviewer know the real you. It is important to know where you're going to focus. If you try to memorize things, there is always the chance that you will lose your place in the middle of your speech, and then you're lost. You will achieve far greater results if you write out your answers and then practice them. Remember, no memorizing allowed. Just be able to tell the story smoothly. If it's not perfect, that's OK. After all, who knows the story better than you?

A New Interview Technique

One of the best techniques I use to help clients answer this type of open-ended question is a Five-Point System. This is a summary to help you prepare and to remember what you want the interviewer to know. This five-point summary becomes your personal brand and should include (1) your education and years of experience, (2) your area of expertise or knowledge, (3) your strengths, (4) your work ethic and reputation, and, if applicable, (5) some personal information (hobbies, interests, volunteer work). What do you want the interviewer to remember about you when you leave?

By writing out your five points before the interview, you will be prepared for a number of questions, because you will have a summary of who you are and what you bring to a position, plus a new tool you are about to learn that will assist you in remembering exactly what you want to tell the interviewer.

The Five-Point System

This system includes *five points* that will not only summarize who you are as a person, but will assist you in staying focused.

- **Point One: Your education and years of experience.**
  This includes any special licenses, certifications, or security clearances. (More experienced persons will talk mainly about experience and not focus on education.

New students will focus on education with special classes or honors received.)

- **Point Two: Your area of expertise.** What do you know a great deal about? This is the information from your knowledge-based skills exercise. It is important to emphasize your experience related to the job posting or description. (People with less experience will have to rely on classes taken or coursework done.)

- **Point Three: Your key strength.** This is usually a trait that you can use in any job. The information from your transferable skills exercise can be used here (i.e., communication skills, relating to others, problem solving, time management).

- **Point Four: Your work ethic or work style.** Refer to your personal traits list. This is what your coworkers would say about you if they were asked. Third-party endorsements work well here.

- **Point Five: Personal facts.** Something interesting about you (a hobby, a volunteer job, a sport or activity that is of interest to you). If you can think of something that relates to the job you are applying for, that would be a plus. Use of personal facts can be an optional point, depending on your circumstances and what you have to say.

The reason the Five-Point System works is because it summarizes in a succinct manner what you have to offer so that you will be less apt to drift off target or forget what you intended to say. Here are some questions that could be answered by using all, or part of the five points:

> Tell me about yourself.
>
> What can you bring to the job that other candidates can't?
>
> What are your strengths?
>
> What makes you unique?
>
> Why should we hire you?
>
> What do others say about you?
>
> Describe your personality.

Writing Your Five Points

By now you've done some significant work if you've been following along with the exercises in the book. It's time to pull all the information together in a format that you can remember easily. Below are exercises for the professional as well as for the student. That is not to say that you can't work on both, if you want the additional practice. You will notice that the student version focuses more on education and extra-curricular activities.

Writing Your Five Points: Professional Version

Point One: Your Education and Experience

Whether you begin your statement with your years of experience or your education will depend on your current status and the position for which you are applying. If you have been working for several years, you will most likely want to focus on your "years of experience," instead of your education, as your experience will become more important if you qualify for the position. You will have to judge your individual situation, as there are some positions that will stress the degrees that are desired. For instance, scientific, medical, and teaching positions, as well as many other professional fields, are interested in your education and training. In those cases, you may decide to start with your education, especially if you have advanced degrees.

Knowledge-based skills: skills you learned from experience and education: computer programs; graphics; languages; writing; training; leadership; science; coaching; sales; special skills; and others.

Statement Examples: Education and Experience

I'll begin with my education, which includes an MBA that I am proud to say I achieved while working full time. I also have a bachelor's degree in accounting and am a certified CPA. Added to that, I have eight years of experience working in the commercial real estate industry.

I have been in the customer service industry for the past four years. My most recent experience has been in the high-tech industry handling incoming calls. In my current job, I formed some significant customer relationships, resulting in a 25 percent increase in sales within a matter of months.

I have been working for the past seven years in the financial banking area. I have had experience and success working in fraud prevention and anti–money laundering. Last year, I stopped three separate fraud cases, saving the bank $100 million. I have been one of the top salespersons at my current position and was rated in the top 10 percent nationwide for sales.

RULE OF THUMB

When you use "quantifiers" and "results" in your examples, the interviewer has a better idea of the scope of responsibility you've dealt with. Use quantifiers, as applicable, both in the interview and on your résumé.

EXERCISE

Your Education and Experience

Fill in the blanks with your own examples.

List your degrees, special training, certifications, overall years of experience, years in a particular type of position, or specialty.

Associate degree:

Bachelor's degree:

Master's degree:

Advanced degree:

Special training/certificates/honors:

Licenses/clearances:

If you have extensive experience at the executive level, this may take precedence over your education. If this is the case, you may want to stress your progressive titles beginning with your most current, or by showing a progression. For example, "I have been in this industry for 10 years, beginning with inside sales, and have progressed through several promotions to district manager, which I have been doing for the past two years." If the interviewer requires more detailed information, he or she will ask.

Experience

Years in the industry/field:

Years of experience in relevant position applying for:
    title

Years of experience in other job titles: title

Current position: title

Summary of responsibility (two to three sentences):

Recognition/awards/accomplishments of interest:

Point Two: Your Area of Expertise

An important factor in any interview is being able to distinguish yourself from the next "guy" who walks through the door. When asked what your area of expertise is, you should immediately think: "knowledge-based skills." These are the skills you acquired from your years of education and experience.

Knowledge-based skills: knowledge of computer programs; graphics; languages; writing; training; management; science; coaching; sales; leadership; special skills, and so on. (These skills were covered in Chapter 2.)

What is your area of expertise? What do you know a great deal about? Are you an SME (subject matter expert)?

Statement Examples: Area of Expertise and Knowledge

My broad experience is my expertise. I have an in-depth knowledge of accounting and finance principles. This knowledge and my analytical ability allow me to work with individuals and to educate them regarding their finances. I have analyzed hundreds of projects to determine their feasibility and then made recommendations as to the effect on others' investments.

My expertise is my problem-solving ability. I am very analytical and computer savvy. I use these skills to view things from a strategic point of view. I have a broad range of experience across multiple retail functional areas with experience in establishing formal planning frameworks to drive growth. Some of my achievements include double-digit cost reduction percentages.

My specialty or area of interest is in internal medicine. I have completed two internships. These experiences have allowed me to learn protocols in the U.S. health-care system and how to build rapport with patients and to deal with different personalities, especially difficult patients.

EXERCISE

Expertise and Knowledge

Fill in the blanks with your own examples.

Business skills/abilities (persuasion, negotiation, managing):

Management skills/abilities (leadership, visionary, forward thinker):

Administrative skills/abilities (project management, coordination, follow through):

Analytical skills/abilities (strategic, analyze, interpret, recommend):

Teaching skills/abilities (knowledgeable, communication, patient):

Mechanical skills/abilities (tools/equipment, maintenance/repairs, skill/craft):

Special training/abilities (pilot's license, inventor, military, law enforcement):

Point Three: Your Key Strengths

Your key strength skills are your transferable skills that you can take with you to any job you hold. Identifying your transferable skills is especially important for anyone who is transferring to another field, or a different type of organization. If you have been out of the workforce and are now re-entering, it will be important to stress these skills, especially if you fall short of experience to meet the qualifications. These are sometimes the skills that many people take for granted without realizing they might distinguish you from the competition.

Transferable skills: skills that are portable such as communication, listening, decision making, judgment, initiative, negotiation, planning, organizing, time management, some leadership skills. (Transferrable skills were covered in Chapter 3.)

Statement Examples: Key Strengths

My strengths are my analytical mind and my research skills, combined with a natural curiosity to find answers. I think the people I have worked with would tell you that they appreciated my skills and my way of thinking through problems.

My strength is my ability to deal with people. This has a lot to do with the fact that I am a good listener and that I'm good at reading people. I have worked with a diversity of people and have always been able to adapt and get along by adjusting my style and vocabulary to meet the person's level.

My strength is my strong leadership ability and style. I believe in being very open in my communications. I work collaboratively with the people who work for and with me. I think my record proves my leadership ability: I was promoted from a staff accountant to a controller, and then to my current position as vice president.

My strength is my ability to solve problems. Throughout my life, it has been something that I have been able to do by looking at the issue and sorting through what is important and what is not important.

EXERCISE

Key Strengths

Fill in the blanks with your own examples.

People skills:

Communication:

Problem solving:

Analytical:

Attention to detail:

Follow-through:

Organized:

Good listener:

Coaching:

Precise:

Thinking out of the box:

Planning:

Scheduling:

Point Four: Your Work Ethic/Loyalty, Achievements

What other traits or experiences would you like the employer to know about you? Your integrity, work ethic, or personal achievements apply here. For example, you achieved a major accomplishment that earned you an award or an honor, or saved the company a great deal of money by thinking of a creative, more efficient solution.

A more comfortable way to talk about your work ethic and personal style is to think about how others see you. Dig out those old performance appraisals and read through those letters of reference for words to use (third-party endorsement)

Question: If I were to ask your coworkers to tell me three positive things about you—your personality, your work style, or what you are like to work with—what would they say?

Statement Examples: Your Work Ethic/Loyalty, Achievements

I have a strong work ethic with an abundance of energy. I can work for hours and days and never tire. I sometimes surprise people who work with me by working for days with no breaks, and being on-call at night.

I consider myself to be very adaptable, and I can usually make friends in new situations. I will go out of my way to help someone who needs help. I try to get to know people on a deeper level.

I am a very hard worker, working an average of 60 to 70 hours a week. I will do whatever it takes to complete a job. I am sure to keep my boss and team workers in the communication loop by setting up time to get their thoughts and their buy-in.

I have a strong work ethic and am very dependable. People who know me and have worked with me would tell you that I am loyal and extremely punctual. They would also tell you that I am fun to be around and that I have a dry sense of humor.

EXERCISE

Work Ethic/Loyalty

Fill in the blanks with your own examples.

Your work ethic/loyalty, achievements:

Performance appraisal quotes:

Comments from past/current bosses:

Comments from your coworkers:

What you perceive your coworkers think of you:

Examples of your work ethic, long hours:

Examples of going above and beyond:

Reference letter comments:

Point Five: Your Personal Traits

Lastly, think of the personal traits that make *you* unique. Depending on your personality and the situation, you may want to talk about some interests or hobbies outside of work. If this feels uncomfortable or inappropriate, then stick to what you've identified as your personal traits.

Don't dismiss these traits as unimportant. More people are fired for negative personal traits than for lack of knowledge.

Personal traits: qualities that make you who you are: flexible; honest; friendly; dependable; decisive; reliable; calm; high energy; patient; good attitude; adaptable; detail oriented. (These traits were covered in Chapter 3.)

Statement Example: Personal Traits

I am a sincere and gentle person. If I sound like I am too serious, I do have a fun side where I like to laugh and make people laugh. My friends would tell you that I have a very funny sense of humor, in appropriate situations.

I have many interests, including music, film, sports, current events, and politics. I have a great sense of humor and can be very witty and sometimes sarcastic. I think something that makes me unique from other candidates is that I am very entrepreneurial. I've been investing in the stock market since I was old enough to drive.

Lastly, I have a very high sense of integrity. My coworkers would describe me as someone who is very dependable and adaptable. They would also tell you that I am a go-getter who is very organized and can take control of chaotic situations when needed.

EXERCISE

Personal Traits

Fill in the blanks with your own examples.
Attitude:
Sense of humor:
Hobbies (especially if connected to the position):
Work style:

Team player:

Energy level:

Interests (news, history, science, etc.):

Confident:

Learning style:

Quiet:

Outgoing:

Formal:

Casual:

Good with people:

Good listener:

Conscientious:

Writing Your Five Points: Student Version

The Five-Point System student version is very similar to the Five-Point System professional version; however, because students typically don't have as much work experience, the words that will be used to describe strengths, skills, and abilities are therefore different. The student, or new grad, for the most part, will rely on "transferable skills" acquired in a variety of ways other than working.

Point One: Your Education and Experience

As a student or recent grad, your education will probably be your strongest starting point unless you have some other relevant experience. If you have work experience of any kind, or have worked as a volunteer or in some other capacity, this exercise will be easier for you because you will have more examples to pull from. If you don't have work experience, you can use your transferable skills to point out the skills you have that you can bring to any job. Any experience is just that: experiences you've had. Experience is what helps you develop skills and should be included in your statement about you and what you have to offer an employer.

For example, if you worked in a retail store or in the fast-food industry, chances are that you have customer service experience. What does it take to have good customer service skills? More than likely it takes people skills. What does it take to have good people skills? It's about relating to others through communication. This could include good interpersonal skills, being patient with people, and problem solving, to name a few traits you may have experienced while working part-time or summers.

If you completed an internship, that is great experience to talk about. This may or may not have been in your area of interest, but it will definitely be something to put on your résumé and be proud of; plus you honed your transferable skills. Also, don't discount any volunteer work you did. You should begin to think about the transferable skills you used or developed in this capacity.

Statement Examples: Education and Experience

To begin, I am in the process of finishing up my BA in finance in December. I have maintained a 4.0 in my major and have been on the Dean's List First Honors four times. During the summer, I have worked for my uncle's construction company.

The area I have excelled in is finance. I have done well in all my finance classes. I really enjoy the material and learning about it. I have always had an aptitude toward math and a head for numbers, and I'm very good at solving problems.

I have worked summers during my college years, and last summer I worked for a high-tech company where I performed a variety of tasks, the most interesting being a data summary analysis condensing huge spreadsheets to manageable categories using Excel.

EXERCISE

Education and Experience

List your degrees, special training, certifications, overall experience, plus any achievements you've had in school or other capacity. Fill in the blanks with your own examples.

Your education: dates of completion or expected
    completion of school:

Associate degree:

Bachelor's degree:

Master's degree:

Advanced degree:

Special training:

Recognition/awards/accomplishments of interest:

GPA:

Dean's list:

Certificates/certifications:

Special classes/study abroad:

School activities:

Honors:

Your experience:

Internship(s):

Work experience:

Summary of responsibility (two to three sentences):

Part-time work:

Full-time work:

Volunteer work experience:

Work published:

Recognition/awards/accomplishments of interest:

School offices held:

Teams or committees:

Societies, fraternities, sororities (office held?):

Point Two: Your Area of Interest (Expertise)

Okay, so maybe you're not an expert yet. But you probably have some areas that you are stronger in than others. Usually when we do well in a subject, or are at least interested in the subject, we tend to do better than with things that are not of interest to us. Here are some questions to ask yourself to determine where your interests are:

> What class have you taken that was of particular interest to you?
> What classes did you like best?
> What classes did you excel in?
> What is your area of expertise?
> What do you know a great deal about?

Select some areas that you have been encouraged to pursue as a career (for example, writing skills, problem solving, math, computers, debate, interpersonal and persuasive skills).

Statement Examples: Area of Expertise (Your Area of Interest or Knowledge)

Math is my strongest point because it comes so easily to me. I understand what is going on right away. I understand the problem and what it will take to get to the solution. This is one reason that investment banking is of interest to me.

Between my work experience and my college classes, I have a good background in basic accounting. In addition, I have taken advanced finance as this is an area of interest to me.

I have been working in the food industry as an assistant manager, managing customers and employees while I have been going to school. I moved quickly up the ranks in the restaurant business and was even offered my own store to manage at one time.

I am very familiar with computers, current technology, and a variety of software and hardware systems. I keep up to date with the latest technology by reading and taking classes. If I don't know an answer to a problem, I know the resources to find it.

EXERCISE

Your Expertise

List the skills and experiences you have that would be required in the type of job you are seeking. For instance, a technical job would focus on programs, languages, and platforms. A public relations job would focus on writing, people skills, and organization. Fill in the blanks with your own examples.

Business skills/abilities (persuasive, negotiation, managing):

Management skills/abilities/offices held in organization/ groups (leadership, visionary, forward-thinker):

Administrative skills/abilities (project management, coordination, follow-through):

Analytical skills/abilities (strategic, analyze, interpret, recommend):

Teaching skills/abilities (knowledgeable, communication, patient):

Mechanical skills/abilities (tools/equipment, maintenance/ repairs, skill/craft):

Special training/abilities (computer certifications, licenses, safety, leadership):

Point Three: Your Key Strengths

You have many strengths, but give some thought to those skills in which you excel. Some people refer to these skills as "soft skills." These skills can be viewed as transferable, meaning you can take them with you to any job. Identifying transferable skills is especially important for students or people with little or no experience. Think about what you have to offer in the way of transferable skills. Chances are that you are probably taking for granted some of the skills that make you unique.

Transferable skills are portable: communication; listening; decision making; judgment; initiative' negotiation; planning; organizing; time management; some leadership skills.

Statement Examples: Strengths

I believe my strengths are my communication/language skills. I communicate with a wide variety of people and am able to adjust my communication style to the audience to whom I am speaking. I am also a good writer.

I have very strong people skills and have worked with a wide diversity of people. I like working with groups where I often become the main "go to guy." I can listen to opposing viewpoints and then become the intermediary, working toward the good of the team.

I consider myself to be very adaptable and usually make friends in new situations. Having worked in a variety of settings during my internships has allowed me to make friends by listening and showing that

I care about other people. I will go out of my way to help someone who needs help.

I would say my strength is my analytical problem solving. My engineering education background has taught me the problem-solving process of planning, troubleshooting, and researching.

EXERCISE

Your Strengths

Fill in the traits where you have excelled. These can be transferable skills or even knowledge-based skills. They may include some personal traits. Fill in the blanks with your own examples.

People skills:

Communication:

Problem solving:

Analytical:

Attention to detail:

Follow through:

Organized:

Good listener:

Coaching:

Precise:

Thinking out of the box:

Planning:

Scheduling:

Point Four: Your Work Ethic/Loyalty, Achievements

What other traits or experiences would you like the employer to know about you? Your integrity, work ethic, or personal achievements would apply here. Maybe some major accomplishment you've had or an honor you received?

One way to determine your work ethic and personal style is to think about how others see you. Think of feedback you've received from others. Think of your interviewer asking your classmates or coworkers to tell him three positive things about you, your personality, and your work style. What if the interviewer asked them what you are like to work with? What would they say?

Statement Examples

I have a strong work ethic and am always ready and willing to volunteer for new projects. I am also very thorough with my research, never leaving any "stone left unturned" when gathering facts. I am easy to work with, and I think my coworkers would describe me as friendly, and willing to help.

I have a very strong work ethic and am known for being someone who is always looking for more work to do. I think my fellow students and project teams would describe me as a "nice guy" who has a lot of respect for others.

I have a lot of energy and know how to channel that energy to get things done on time. I am extremely organized and efficient with time management. I have been able to work part-time, get good grades, and participate as a member of the college band.

EXERCISE

Your Work Ethic/Loyalty, Achievements

Fill in the blanks with your own examples.

Comments/quotes from teachers/professors:

Comments from fellow students:

Feedback from any coworkers or bosses — part-time/
  voluntary work:

What you perceive your fellow students think
  about you:

Examples of your work ethic, long hours:

Examples of going above and beyond:

Comments on grades:

Reference letter comments:

Point Five: Your Personal Traits, Personality

Lastly, think of the personal traits that make *you* unique. Maybe you are very organized, punctual, and never miss deadlines, or perhaps you are willing to go above and beyond what is asked or have a great, upbeat attitude.

(Don't dismiss these traits as unimportant. More people are fired for negative personal traits than for lack of knowledge.)

Personal traits: qualities that make you who you are: flexible; highly moral; friendly; dependable; decisive; reliable; calm; high energy; patient; good attitude; adaptable; detail oriented.

RULE OF THUMB

Personal traits cannot be taught, even though some employers would like to. They should be valued as important to the total picture of who you are.

Statement Examples: Personal Traits

Something personal about me is that I am an entrepreneur. While going to college, I started my own export company where I deal daily with customers and employees.

I have a good sense of humor and can make hard, tedious work fun and easy using funny stories to get my point across.

I have many interests including music, film, sports, current events, and politics. I have a great sense of humor and can be very witty and sometimes sarcastic.

EXERCISE

Your Personal Traits, Personality

Fill in the blanks with your own examples.

Attitude:

Sense of humor/fun:

Hobbies (especially if connected to the position):

Work style:

Team player:

Energy level:

Interests (news, history, science, etc.):

Confident:

Learning style:

Quiet:

Outgoing:

Formal:

Casual:

Good with people:

Good listener:

Conscientious:

Examples of the Five Points

Point One: Education and Experience

I have a BS in computer science and have been working in the IT industry for the past five years. I have diverse experience working for small companies as well as Fortune 500 companies. I am currently a senior analyst consultant and have been for the past three years.

Point Two: Your Area of Expertise

My area of expertise is that I am a subject matter expert for the company's technology. I am also knowledgeable about many other computer languages, programs, and applications.

Point Three: Your Key Strength

My strength is my strong interpersonal skills. I am able to work with a diverse group of people in various ranks within the company. I adjust my style and vocabulary according to who I am speaking to ranging from executives to outside vendors. I try to use language that they will understand without getting too technical and talking down to them.

Point Four: Your Work Ethic, Loyalty

I am a person who works well in stressful situations without getting frustrated. I consider myself even-keeled, and I work well with others. I think my coworkers would describe me as personable and fun to work with. I try to stay lighthearted and can usually find something to joke about, especially in tense situations.

Point Five: Your Personal Info, as Appropriate

On the personal side, I am into physical fitness. I work out five to six times a week, running and lifting weights. I also like the outdoors, and hiking is something I do with my friends every year. But, you can usually find me in front of the TV when there's a good football game on.

End with something about you being there at the company for an interview and what it means to you, or why you think you are an excellent fit for the position. Keep it brief, but it's good to have an ending transition:

> As you can hear, I am a good fit for this position's requirements. I have been very impressed with what I have experienced by going through your hiring process and hope that you consider me a serious candidate.

Example: Complete Statement for a Professional

I'm the kind of person who keeps one eye on the future while taking care of today's business. I know how to get things done, but at the same time I have the ability to foresee areas that may become problems and put processes in place to prevent the problems from occurring.

I have been in business operations for more than seven years. My experience has been broad in that I have been very successful in developing ways to improve businesses and make them more profitable. I've worked in a number of companies in various industries, banking, retail, and the medical fields, and transitioned seamlessly to each.

I believe my success can be attributed to my strong leadership and decision-making style. I talk to employees and managers and share the goals so that everyone is on the same page. I work with the underachievers and put process improvements in place. I work with management to develop budgets that can be attained.

I would describe my style as open and honest. I share all pertinent information with the employees one-on-one and listen to their ideas, concerns, desires, and needs. I teach them to utilize resources and tools and provide feedback so that they realize their contribution to the organization.

When I look at your job posting, I can see myself in the role, bringing my vast knowledge and record of success in improving processes. I am very enthusiastic about your company and know that I could bring my creative and problem-solving ability to this job.

Example: The Complete Statement for a Student

I am a fourth-year computer engineering major. I have taken an indirect path to what I really want to do, which is to work in finance. I feel that I have added value to offer by bringing the two disciplines together.

Math is my strongest point. I understand what is going on right away. As an example, in physics I see the big picture, where some people need lots of examples. I get it very quickly and understand the problem and what it will take to get to the solution. This is one reason that investment banking is of interest to me.

Between my part-time work experience and my college classes, I have a good background in basic accounting. In addition, I have taken advanced finance, as this is an area of interest.

I have been working in the food industry as an assistant manager, managing customers and employees while I have been going to school. The people I supervise have given me great feedback about my management style and they would ask for me to be their supervisor if they had a choice. I have moved quickly up the ranks in the restaurant business, and now feel I have a basic understanding of the issues facing clients in the business sector.

These statements can range from two minutes to four minutes, depending on the situation. If you are prepared, you can adapt your statement as appropriate. If your interviewer seems in a hurry or is checking his watch, that would be a clue to shorten your statement.

I hope you can see that there are many benefits to working through the exercises and writing your five points. A little work can result in a smooth, concise answer to any open-ended question about you. The more work that you put into these exercises, the more succinct and prepared you will be for your next interview. Remember, these are not answers to memorize, but to walk through from point to point.

Bringing It All Together: Template

Using the template below will make summarizing your five points easier. Using the work you've completed in the previous exercise, you will transfer each of the points into one concise document. This document will then be summarized to answer open-ended questions about you and what you have to offer an employer.

Think of this as a working document that can be changed and rewritten for each job you apply for, if needed. These points are the basics of what you want the interviewer to know about you.

Your Five Points Template

Point One: Start with education and experience as identified in the exercise.

Point Two: Next, your area of "expertise" as identified in the exercise.

Point Three: Write your key strength/"transferable skills" as identified in the exercise.

Point Four: Experiences you'd like the employer to know about you, which were identified in the exercise.

Point Five: Your "personal traits" as identified in the exercise.

The Statement

After you have finished writing your five points, take a step back and start to think of how you will say them. Since we write more formally than we talk, they should be put in a less formal speech format. You want your "voice" and style to come through. This statement should *not* sound like something that you've memorized, or you will come off sounding like a recording.

A Tool To Remember: Your Five Points and Your Five Fingers

How can you possibly remember all those points? While you can't bring a "cheat sheet" into the interview, you can bring your fingers. You can use your fingers as a tool to help you to stay focused. Use each finger as a talking point:

The thumb (strong base): education and experience.

The pointer finger (directed): your expertise or knowledge of the job.

The middle finger (to the point): your strength—transferable or personal.

The ring finger (loyalty): people skills, communication, "whatever it takes" attitude.

The little finger (weakest): personal information that is engaging and interesting about you, or how the combination of all these traits together makes you unique.

The five finger method is a technique that has helped my clients not only stay focused but assisted them when they lost track of where they were headed. Here are statements received from clients after their interviews:

> *The five points for five fingers worked like a charm. I must have had a brain freeze, because I went blank and almost panicked, then I remembered my five points and the five fingers exercise and I just grabbed the wheel for dear life and went through them, point-by-point.*

What helped me tremendously and pulled me out of a few scary moments were my five fingers. I am so glad that I learned that technique. It saved the day.

Whether you use the five finger method to remember or some other method, you should be prepared to answer the question, "Tell me about yourself." Even if it isn't asked in that format, you will benefit from having your information organized so you can easily remember it. Think of it as your sales "brochure" about yourself; you are the product. It will make a difference in the way that you present yourself, as well as in your ability to talk openly without being modest about what you have to offer. You will be able to tell the interviewer why he should hire you, and what makes you unique.

Is There Anything Else You'd Like to Add?

There are times at the end of the interview when you may be asked, *"Is there anything else you'd like to add?"* This is an invitation for you to sum up what you can bring. Use your five points as a quick summary at the end of the interview.

Interviewer's question: "Is there anything else you'd like to add?"
Candidate's answer: "Before I leave I would like to summarize what I would bring to the job."

Remember, this is a summary. If you decide to do a brief summary, it should be no more than one minute. Do not belabor what you've already told the interviewer; you're just hitting the high spots to remind him or her of what you have to offer and why you are the best person for the job. Points one, two, three, four, and five, summarized in a quick, succinct manner.

CHAPTER 6

Your Examples and Stories

The Behavioral Interview

Behavioral interviewing is not new. In fact, it's has been around since the 1970s when industrial psychologists developed a way they said would accurately predict whether a person would succeed in a job. They concluded that if candidates were asked questions that required specific examples of past behavior, it would be an indicator of their future behavior. Employers then began using this interviewing technique to determine whether a candidate was a good fit for the job. The technique is of growing interest to companies who would like to choose the "right" candidate, especially in today's market with so many candidates to choose from.

The difference between a behavioral question and other questions is that a behavioral question will be very specific about asking for an example. An interviewer who is using behavioral questions would ask: "Tell me about a time when you solved a problem by taking the initiative." The key words are "a time." The answer asks for a "specific" example of a time or "specific" incident.

Behavioral questions *always* require an example of a specific incident. The following are some examples of this type of question:

- Tell me about a time when...
- Can you give me an example of...
- Describe a situation when...
- Recall a time that...
- Tell me how you achieved this accomplishment on your résumé?
- You say that you have good ... skills. Give me an example of when those skills made a difference in the outcome of a situation.
- You say you're a "hard worker." Can you give me an example?
- I see on your résumé you accomplished ... for your last company. Describe how you did this.

There is a pattern to the questions regardless of the subject, and you will notice that they are very specific to an incident. The first thing to practice is listening to the interview question and then deciding whether it's a behavioral question that requires an example or it's a situational question that requires your thinking process. The next thing to think about is, what's behind the question being asked? What factor is the interviewer seeking with this particular question?

Behavioral Questions vs. General or Situational Questions

When an interviewer asks only general, hypothetical, or situational questions, the interview falls short of flushing out details and the interviewer will fail to get good examples from the candidate. While this is not your problem, you may be able to help a "weak interviewer" by giving him or her examples that will impress and therefore increase your chances of getting the job.

In an interview in which the interviewer is asking general or hypothetical questions only, a candidate might say: "I have excellent communication skills." Without an example of these communication skills, the interviewer will have to take the candidate's word for the claim. Or, even worse, judge the candidate on how the candidate is communicating in the interview. You can see that this isn't the best way for you to prove you have excellent communication skills because you may feel under some pressure and possible duress.

An interviewer who is using behavioral interview questions and techniques would ask a follow-up question if someone claimed to have excellent communication skills: "You say that you have excellent communication skills. Tell me about a time when these skills made a difference in the outcome of a situation."

(Possible factors: negation skills; communication; conflict resolution; persuasion.)

Or, the interviewer could ask: "Give me an example of a time when you had a conflict with a coworker and what you did about it."

(Possible factors: communications; relating to others; calm in difficult situations; listening skills; problem solving skills.)

Or, another example: "One of the most important aspects of this job is selling. Can you give me an example of a time when you convinced someone to buy when they were quite resistant to making a purchase?"

(Possible factors: communication; persuasion; problem solving; negotiation.)

When those follow-up questions are asked, they become behavioral questions that will require an example of a time when a specific incident happened that involved your communication skills. In order to answer this type of question, you must be able to give an example or tell a story of a time when these excellent communication skills made a difference. If you cannot do this, your claim is weakened or doubted. Think about this technique as if an interviewer is saying to you: "Okay, you say you have excellent communication skills. Prove it."

While preparation is important for every interview, it is essential to prepare for the behavioral interview. You must have examples and stories for anything you have claimed on your résumé or that you say in an interview.

RULE OF THUMB

Never say anything on a résumé or in an interview that you can't stand behind with an example or a story.

This technique is a successful way for the interviewer to begin piecing together patterns of behavior. If the interviewer is not using behavioral questions, you could ask if he or she would be interested in hearing your example. You could say, "I have actually done that (or had that happen), and I can provide you with an example." Sometimes the interviewer will be interested in hearing your example, but there will be times when the interviewer is short of time and does not want to hear your example. Let your instincts guide you on when to offer an example if you are not asked for one.

Techniques for Writing Your Examples and Stories

Now, the question is: "How do I get ready for this type of interview?" Preparing your stories before the interview will take the mystique out of behavioral interviewing and allow you to tell the success stories you want your interviewer to hear. Through your examples, the interviewer will begin to get a clear picture of you, and as a result will be able to decide whether you are the right person for the job based on your past experience and successes.

In order to successfully give an example and answer a behavioral question, you must first learn a technique to assure that your example will convey the message you want to send. This technique involves your ability to tell a good story. Unfortunately, not everyone is a natural-born storyteller. But the good news is by learning some simple rules and formulas, you too can become a storyteller who can relate your experiences as proof of what you have claimed in an interesting manner.

To begin with the lesson in storytelling you must first learn the proportions of a good story. The following is a fun fairy tale that I use with my clients to demonstrate how *not* to tell a story.

The Fractured Fairy Tale

Think of a young child coming to you and asking you to tell her a story. You don't consider yourself a great storyteller, but you're willing to give it a try.

123

Once upon a time there was a beautiful princess, and she was locked in the tower of a building. The building was 14 stories high, and was made of white stucco. The weather was mild and there were lots of white puffy clouds. She was wearing a red dress and had blonde hair and brown eyes. She was very sad to be locked in a tower.

One day, a prince happened to ride by on his horse. He saw the lovely princess and asked why she was crying. She told him that she was a prisoner and wanted to go home. The prince told her that he would rescue her.

But alas, the tower was being guarded by a big, green dragon. The dragon had fiery breath, and was very scary.

So, what the prince did next was go in and slay the dragon. He killed him dead and stepped over him to get to the tower. He climbed the tower stairs and got the princess out.

And, that's the end of the story.

"Oh no," the child says. "That can't be the end. I want to hear more. I don't care about the building, or the puffy clouds, or what the princess was wearing. What I *want to know* is how the prince killed the dragon. And, I *want to know* what happened after he freed the princess. Did they live happily ever after? Did they go their separate ways? What happened?"

Your listener is upset and wants more details, and not the ones that you provided so far.

You can see that your storytelling techniques leave something to be desired with this story. But, the good news is that it was your first attempt, so there's hope. We are about to explore a technique that will teach you how to become a first-class storyteller.

How To Tell a Good Story

Let's try again, and this time take the story from a different slant. Try thinking of storytelling as if you were describing a movie. Most movies start out by setting the scene. This would be the first five minutes of a movie, more or less. So, with some guidelines, we'll try telling that fairy tale again to see if it makes a difference.

Twenty Percent of a Story Is Setting the Scene: Beginning

It is important to explain where you are when this story takes place.

> *There was a lovely princes trapped in a high tower in a dark forest.*

Next, tell what your role was.

> (Assuming you are the prince) *I happened along and saw this beautiful young woman trapped in a tower who was upset and asking for my help.*

What was the problem?

> *I immediately wanted to assist her, but there was a big, ugly dragon guarding the tower, and so far no one had figured out how to get past him to get the princess out.*

Although the example has details, there is no need to talk about "puffy clouds." In other words, give the detailed facts that are important to the story, but don't dwell on the unimportant details such as the color of her dress or her eyes.

This is the formula for dealing with the beginning of any story, the first 20 percent. As the listener, I now have an idea of the setup: you are the prince, and the beautiful princess is in trouble. I know that in order to solve the problem you are going to have to deal with the dragon. The question is: How?

Sixty Percent of the Story Is the Action: What Happened?

It is now time to move into the action of the story. This is the plot of a movie where you, as the star, should give the listener the details of what took place and what you did.

"The first thing I did was ..." (By using this phrase, or one like it, you are signaling the *action* of the story. The plot is now beginning.)

> *I carefully walked around the dragon, making sure that he did not see me. I then considered my options. Being a natural-born problem solver, I saw that I would have an advantage if I were to attack him from above.*
>
> *So I climbed the tallest tree I could find. Next, I tied a piece of meat to a string and threw it out to see if he was hungry. He immediately took the bait and ate the meat; he was hungry. The next piece of meat I coated with poison. (A good prince always carries a bit of poison.)*

I set up a strategy where I would throw the poisoned meat and then jump onto his back while he was distracted. This was risky, but I evaluated the situation and saw that it was possible. I threw out a big piece of meat, and it worked great. The dragon immediately went for the poison-laced meat, and I made my move. I jumped onto his back, and he didn't even notice.

Next, I pulled out my sword and aimed carefully for the dragon's heart. I made a direct hit the first time. The dragon roared and bucked, but I held on as tightly as I could. I rode that dragon for about 15 minutes.

The whole time I was scared he would throw me to the ground and eat me as quickly as he had eaten the meat. But I was determined. About this time the poison was starting to take effect and the dragon was getting tired. Eventually, he fell over dead, and I was able to climb to safety.

The listener is now caught up in the story. You are a hero, and he is impressed with your story and your determination. He also sees that you are a problem solver who is willing to take a risk. This is all good.

Twenty Percent of a Story Is the Ending: The Result

If you leave a movie five minutes early, you will never know the end of the story or how it turned out. The same holds true of giving an example in an interview. Many storytellers forget that this is an important part of the story.

I was able to climb over the dragon and climb the tower stairs to free the princess. She was very grateful and asked me to take her home to her father, the king. When we arrived at the palace, there was much celebrating. The king and queen were so happy to see their daughter unharmed. They couldn't thank me enough. The king insisted on giving me a place in his ranks as a knight. He said, "You have the qualities I've been looking for as a guard for my daughter." He also told me he was impressed with my problem-solving skills and actions. (Good third-party endorsement here.) *From that day forward I have faithfully taken care of the princess and kept her safe from all dragons.*

The End.

You can now appreciate the difference in the two stories and how using the right details in the right places can emphasize the factor you are going after. The possible factors in this case are problem solving; evaluating a situation; decision making; action-oriented.

Job interviewing isn't about fairy tales, but it is about telling interesting stories. Can you imagine sitting and listening to poorly told stories all day long? That's what most interviewers are faced with when they interview unprepared candidates. And then, along you come with your interesting, well-prepared stories, and you're like a breath of fresh air. It pays to tell a good story.

Show, Don't Tell

The secret to doing well at storytelling in a behavioral interview is showing the interviewer what you did, not just telling him or her. By using details to tell your story, you prevent your stories from being flat and uninteresting and sometimes even boring, and your stories become fun and informative.

A good example of telling is saying, "I was very angry."

The way to show with the words is to say, "I stormed into the room, slammed the door, and threw my books on the table."

Now you have visually described your actions and made them more colorful and impressionable.

Proportions Count

The number one mistake made in behavioral interviewing is in the proportions of the story. Most people tend to focus on the problem, when they should focus on the action. There are several methods and acronyms used in various books that describe the formatting of stories, but the main point to remember is that there are three key elements to any story:

1. A beginning: "There was a time..."
2. A middle: "The action steps I took were..."
3. An ending: "The end result was..."

When you add proportions to your storytelling, you have a tool to assist you in shaping your stories:

- A beginning of 20 percent
- A middle of 60 percent
- An ending of 20 percent

Behavioral Story Examples

Question: "Tell me about a time when you solved a problem by thinking creatively."

Example 1: A Story That Does Not Answer the Question

I usually keep up with what's going on in the general market, and sometimes have to act fast to get market share. We were trying to get attention in a fast-paced environment. I spent a great deal of work around budget, attempting to maximize leverage. I've been known to buy some premium advertising to get the word out. I've led some pretty successful campaigns, even when market conditions have not been in our favor.

The problem is that this answer does not address the question. There is no specific project cited. It is a lot of general information that doesn't tell the interviewer anything about you as the candidate specifically. The structure is out of proportion without a beginning, a middle, and an end. It's a story that just rambles.

Example 2: A Story That Does Not Answer the Question
Problem: 20 percent

When I started at my last company, there was a problem with customer retention. I was a supervisor and decided to do something about the problem. I knew that if I teamed with my staff as well as several other

*key players in relevant departments, we could change
this situation.*

Action: 60 percent

*The first thing I did was hold a meeting with my staff,
and we brainstormed ideas. I then formed teams to go
out and interview customers. This was the first time
the company had done this type of research. When
the data was collected, I compiled a spreadsheet and
spent hours calculating the results. All of this was in
addition to my regular duties.*

*After analyzing the spreadsheet, I was able to
come up with a plan to satisfy customer needs with
the idea that satisfied customers tend to come back.*

*I presented the plan to the key players in the
marketing department, and they were able to improve
the plan by changing some of the steps we were planning. I worked closely with the marketing team to col-
laborate a plan of action.*

*The key to the success of this program was get-
ting buy in from my team. I was able to accomplish
this by including them from the beginning.*

Result: 20 percent

*We ended up with a successful strategy to change the
way we were communicating with customers. The plan
was very successful, and my goal was accomplished.
I was given much praise from upper management as
well as kudos from my staff members.*

This is a good answer because it gives an example of a specific project. The question asks for "a time when you solved a problem with creative thinking." With this answer the interviewer can hear the action steps taken and the leadership role you demonstrated. There are many factors that surface in this story: leadership, initiative, teamwork, strategic thinking, analysis and problem solving, and thinking out of the box. This example of past behavior is a good indicator of what your future success could be. From this answer you appear to be a person that has the ability to work as a leader, working with the smaller details while maintaining the "big picture" prospective. If you did it before you can do it again.

RULE OF THUMB

While preparation is important for every interview, it is essential to prepare for the behavioral interview.

You must have examples or stories for any statement that you have claimed on your résumé or that you say in an interview. Preparing your stories before the interview will take the mystique out of behavioral interviewing and allow you to tell the success stories you want your interviewer to hear and see. By showing the interviewer what you have done, you will enable him to get a clear picture of you and whether you are the right person for the job based on your past experience and successes.

Who's Your Costar?

You are always the star of your stories told in answering behavioral questions; it's about you and what you did. But, sometimes your stories will require a "costar." It is difficult to have a conflict with yourself. By describing your costar—even giving him or her a name—you will show who you are dealing with. There is a big difference if you are having a conflict with a six-foot, five-inch bully, or a five-foot, two-inch female who has a possible problem.

Example of a Story with a Costar

Problem:

I had been working at XYZ Company for five years, and I was asked to lead a new project that involved input from five people. I was conducting the kickoff meeting, and one of the team members, Bill, was making faces and shaking his head while I spoke. I thought, "He's not on board." I kept my focus and communicated each person's responsibilities. After the meeting, I knew I was going to have to meet with Bill to find out what the problem was. Bill is an older guy and had a lot more experience than I had. I needed his contributions, but his attitude was going to sink the team's morale. I knew I had to do something immediately.

Action:

The first thing I did was I called Bill and asked if he could come by my office. The minute he walked

133

through the door and plopped down in a chair, I could see I had a problem. He sat there with his arms folded and didn't make eye contact.

I said, "Bill, I know you're wondering why we are having this meeting."

He replied in a very sarcastic tone, "Yeah I am. I have a ton of work to do, and this project is a big deal."

I nodded and said, "Listen, I completely agree. It is a key project for all of us. What I'm wondering is what's going on that's making you upset about your responsibilities in this effort?" He snapped back immediately, "No, no, you're the one in charge here. They made you the lead, and those are your responsibilities."

I realized Bill was definitely feeling resentment toward me because I was asked to lead this project and not him. I sat back in my chair for a few seconds and replied, "Thank you for your time and your candor. I respect someone who tells me the truth. I'm also not here to boss you around. Teamwork is very important to me."

He responded, "Well, I didn't get the role I wanted, and yeah, I'm not thrilled about it."

I had hit a nerve. I replied, "Okay, let's talk about it. Tell me what's on your mind. Your opinion matters to me."

Bill was definitely bitter and said, "I've got more experience than you or anyone else on the project. But who cares about that, right?"

I replied right away, "Bill, you are the key guy on this project. You know the work best, and your ideas do matter. Let's talk about what can be better, and what should be different. Bill, I am serious. I want to hear it."

He uncrossed his arms for the first time and looked me directly in the eye. His expression brightened, and he began to talk. We talked for an hour that day, each of us getting excited about the ideas he was sharing.

Result:

At the end of a long hour, Bill said, "I really apologize, and I wasn't trying to be rude to you. This is a really big project, and it matters. I just didn't feel like I was being heard."

I said, "Well, I heard you. Everything you said. And we can start putting these ideas into work. Open communication is very important to me. My door is always open."

Following our meeting, Bill's attitude completely changed. He brought up several more ideas that have been useful to the project. One of the managers even came to me and said that my team members, especially Bill, seemed really motivated. He was impressed with our teamwork. Since then I've worked productively with Bill on several other projects.

This is a great example of conflict with a coworker. Getting a picture of "Bill" and the way he was behaving, including his body language, helped the listener realize that the interviewee was dealing with a senior person who had some attitude. The story shows good communication and relating to others, but also shows leadership and motivation skills.

By describing Bill in more detail, the interviewee also showed maturity in handling difficult situations and individuals, as well as taking the initiative to take action when something was not right.

Examples of Behavioral Questions and Answers

As you read through these answers, see if you can pick out the reasons that one answer is stronger than another answer. See if you can identify which stories follow the guidelines and give detail where necessary and follow the proportions of good storytelling. Also, you can see that it is most important to answer the question asked. Listening skills count when you're interviewing.

Question: "Tell me about the biggest project you've worked on from start to finish."
(Possible key factors: planning and organizing; time management; teamwork.)

> (**A**) *The company I worked for received a huge order. In fact, it was the biggest order the company ever achieved. The order was for a major client, and the completion of the order would be a major bonus for us and become a revenue stream for the future. Our challenge was a pricing issue. To design what we set out to design became unreasonable because of the cost of*

materials and labor. After many meetings we were able to combine some of the features of the product and still satisfy the customer. I never worked harder on a project to meet an unrealistic expectation.

This is a weak answer because it puts too much emphasis on the company and the project and not enough on "your" role. What exactly was your role in this team effort? Where is the planning and organizing? One of the biggest mistakes candidates make is not saying what their role was and adding more details of actions taken.

(B) *We had a safety project that most of us had little or no prior experience with. We really had to pull together and share information and resources to pull this one off. Fortunately, we all got along well and supported one another. We were able to put together this project with a lot of effort. We stayed late and worked weekends for two months. We worked closely with the other dements in the company to make sure we were meeting the customers' needs. The good news is that we were able to get it done. Everybody felt really good about pulling together on this one.*

There is a definite problem with this answer. There are too many "we's" (seven to be exact) and not enough "I's" (none). As the answer stands, the interviewer has no idea what "your" role was. While it is important to give credit where credit is due, it is also necessary to describe what you did to pull this project together as a team member or leader.

(C) *I was in charge of designing the safety program for a huge order received by my last company. The first thing I did was to select three top technicians to work with me. We worked as a team, with each of us assigned a piece of the project. I led the group by coordinating the schedules and making sure all the deadlines were met. I was in constant communication with my team members and was there to troubleshoot as needed. Because of the open communication between the four of us, we were able to complete the project ahead of the shipping date.*

This is a strong answer because it gives a very clear picture, with details of the situation. Even though this was a team situation, the interviewer is able to see "your" role in solving the problem. By using the pronoun "I," you give a clearer picture of the skills you used. This example talks about some of the skills you used. That includes key factors: leadership, coordinating, follow-through, tracking, communication, problem solving, time management, and troubleshooting.

Question: "Describe a time when you had to adapt to a new situation."
(Possible key factors: adaptable; flexible; make changes.)

(A) *I've become quite accustomed to new situations in the IT industry. I've been laid off twice in the last five years. In fact, one of the companies closed the doors as we walked out. I've had to accept the fact that not all start-up companies are going to make it.*

This answer doesn't show how you adapted to something that was within your control. It is not a bad answer because there was adapting to a new job when you were laid off, but you did not adapt to a situation in which your actions would have made a difference.

This answer is more about accepting and moving on than it is adapting. Anyone can get laid off and adapt to not getting a paycheck, but what you did to take control of a situation is more important.

> **(B)** *My military background has prepared me for this part of any job. When you have been on call day and night and responsible for your unit's safety, you learn to be adaptable and flexible. Being flexible in the service is not only necessary, it is mandatory. I bring that same set of skills and sense of urgency to any job. I do whatever it takes to get the job done.*

While this is a good example, it is a mediocre answer because it does not give an example of a specific time. You show a sense of adaptability and that you have experience responding to new and unexpected situations, but what is missing is a specific example to ensure that this is not talk with no action. In other words, can you do it again?

> **(C)** *I was on call 24/7 one weekend, and when the phone rang on Sunday morning, I knew there was a problem. Sure enough, there was a mainframe that had gone down. The first thing I did was to cancel my plans for the day. I responded to the call within one*

hour. I teamed up with three technicians to get the system up and running before morning. We each had a responsibility but worked as a unit. We stayed until 2:00 a.m. When the employees arrived at work that morning, no one was aware there had been a problem. We got high kudos for responding so quickly.

This is a strong answer because it answers the question with a specific example of adapting to a situation. It allows the interviewer to hear how flexible you are when you describe canceling plans and getting to the scene within an hour. This answer also shows how well you work with others. Your willingness to stay until 2:00 a.m. should convince the interviewer that you are dedicated to getting the job done.

Question: "Your résumé states that you're a 'hard worker.' Can you give me an example of a time when you worked hard?"
(Possible factors: motivation; initiative; punctual; meets deadlines.)

(A) *I always try to get the work done on time. Sometimes that means working overtime. Sometimes I can't get all my work done during the day and I'm willing to stay late to finish up. There have been times when I just couldn't get everything done no matter how hard I worked. I always do my best to meet deadlines, but sometimes you just have to let go. I'd rather do it right and be late than do it wrong and be on time.*

This is a weak answer because it does not include an example of working hard and emphasizes meeting deadlines, which is not quite the same skill. The interviewer could get the idea that you miss deadlines and have a difficult time keeping up with the workload. This answer needs to emphasize the times you stayed late and why the workload was too big to handle.

> **(B)** *I am a very hard worker. I am always punctual and get my work done. The tighter the deadline is, the harder I work. I plan my day so that I'm never late with my work, and I always meet deadlines. If you asked my last boss, he would tell you what a hard worker I am. I do whatever I have to do to get the job done.*

This answer provides all the right traits: motivation; initiative; punctual; meets deadlines; but no examples of using those traits in an actual situation. This answer does benefit from the endorsement from your boss. Bringing the boss into the story is a great way to strengthen the story (third-party endorsement).

> **(C)** *In my recent job, my boss had a really important project, and it didn't look like we were going to make the deadline. I volunteered to do some late nights and weekends. My boss and two other coworkers worked seven straight days with no time off. My piece of the project was to coordinate all the*

information and enter the data. It was a real team effort, but we were able to meet the deadline. My boss was extremely pleased, and he rewarded us all for our efforts.

This is a strong answer because it gives a specific example of going "above and beyond" what was expected. Some of the skills that appear in this answer are initiative, teamwork, coordination skills, a great attitude, a cooperative spirit, and a willingness to make the boss look good.

Question: "Can you give me an example of working in a fast-paced environment?"
(Possible factors: adaptable; speed; handles stressful situations; organized.)

(A) I thrive in fast-paced environments where I am challenged to meet deadlines. The more pressure there is, the better I respond. I have been involved in as many as five projects at the same time, all with tight deadlines. I always learn from each project I accomplish and can apply the new information to the next project to be more efficient. I have the ability to think very quickly and respond to situations as needed, with a good sense of what is needed. I've never had an assignment when I haven't had success. I have very good organizational skills and communication skills. I also have great computer skills that can help with the tracking of a project.

This answer does not give any specific examples. You say that you "have very good organizational and communications skills." Prove it. Give an example. Anybody can say that he or she is good at any task, but when you give a specific example of a time when you did the task, the interviewer gets a better idea of how you worked in the past, which is an indicator of future success.

> **(B)** *When I was a support person in a law office, there was one time when we had to get everything ready for a case and were short-staffed because one of the other support persons was out ill. I took on the responsibility of coordinating all the reports. The first thing I did was sit down with the attorneys involved and ask them to give me an idea of the priorities that they needed to complete their projects. I then put together a task spreadsheet and worked with everyone to keep on track. We worked late into the night, but instead of being tired, I felt energized throughout the experience. It was really rewarding when we finished the last task and made the deadline. Everyone was really surprised at how smoothly it went with all the obstacles I had to work around. I received a nice bonus for my efforts.*

This is a strong answer because it provides a very good example of working in a fast-paced environment, which is what the question was about. It also shows a good attitude of pitching in and getting something done. This example points out organizational skills, initiative, leadership, judgment, the ability to communicate, and a willingness to do "whatever it takes to get the job done."

(C) *We had this project to work on, and it seemed like everything was going wrong. First of all, we had a very tight deadline and were short a staff member. We had handled this type of pressure before, but this case was a particularly important case because it was one of our major clients. This case included a lot of visuals, such as charts and graphs and photos. The attorneys were really under a lot of pressure, and there was a lot of tension in the office. At one point I just felt like sitting down and crying, but I didn't. I just kept working through the anxiety and tension. I knew that if we didn't get this pulled together in time, there would be a very dissatisfied client. We all worked overtime that weekend, but we completed the job on time.*

This answer does not reveal any of your skills. There is too much emphasis on the problem without an explanation of your role. There are too many "we's" and not enough "I's." The only direct reference to your behavior is when you talk about how stressed you were: "I just felt like sitting down and crying." The positive is that you said, "But I didn't," which indicates that you are not a quitter and that you have perseverance.

Who Is "We"?

Pronouns can be troublesome little things.

There is no "I" in team.

I have heard this from clients who worried about claiming credit for a project that was done by a team where they were one of the members. I understand that part. But when you use "we" too many times in a story, I have no idea what your part of the team project was. Even if you were on a team, you had a specific role.

Think of it as if you were on a football team.

You tell me: "My team won the game this weekend. We made five touchdowns."

What part of "we" were you? Did you carry the ball over the goal line? Were you the quarterback and passed the ball? Were you on the defense, holding back the other team players? Were you sitting on the bench? Were you the coach?

Can you see how "we" does not define *your* part in the story?

If you tell me: "My team won the game this weekend. We made five touchdowns and I was the one who was able to carry the ball across the goal line twice. What a great feeling that was! One of my teammates told me he was with me all the way."

Now you're cooking! It's about *your role* on the team.

Question: "Can you give us an example of a time when you were able to convince others to change things your way?" (Possible factors: communication, negotiations, relate to others, motivation.)

(A) *My current boss is not very receptive to new ideas. I was able to sell her on one of my ideas when I showed her a marketing plan that I worked on to change some of the channels we were using for distribution. Behind the scenes I put together a lot of data and analysis that included details, facts, and figures. That extra effort really paid off when I presented her with the idea. She is one of those people who need facts to make decisions. She trusted me a lot more after that.*

This is not a bad answer, but it could be strengthened by more detail. Describing the analytic process and the types of facts and figures that you found and presented would have made the story stronger. The best part of this answer is your ability to understand that your boss has a style, which requires facts, and your ability to adapt your approach to meet her needs.

(B) *My boss would tell you that I am always selling him on ideas. I have at least one idea a week. Some work, and some don't. My success rate is about 75 percent positive. One of the frustrations that I have is getting through the approval stage. When you work for a large company, it sometimes can take weeks to get an idea through the mill. I am an action-oriented guy who wants to make things happen. Sometimes it takes so long to get an idea through the channels that it is less effective than it would be if I had been able to start on it when I first had the idea.*

This answer is too general, and it provides no facts. It starts out well with a 75 percent success rate, but then proceeds to complain about the company and dealing with the process. Since this may not be the way that this company handles such information, it is best to ask questions about the process first and then judge whether this culture is going to be different from the one you just left.

(C) *Recently, I determined a need to market a product by using a different strategy. I met with my boss to convince her of my ideas, and she reluctantly gave me the go-ahead. I then met with the editorial, creative, and media departments. Working together, we planned media exposure, including TV, radio, print, newspaper, and interactive. We also put together a direct mail campaign. I calculated expenses and return on investment and presented it to my boss for approval. I really surprised her with the numbers and my estimated 30 percent return on investment. She gave a "thumbs-up" to proceed with the project. The result was absolutely great. We not only had a dynamite success, but we saved more than $50,000 costs.*

This is a strong answer because of the example it gives of action on your part. The story parts are laid out: the situation, the action you took, the results. Showing a positive outcome makes for a good success story. There are times, however, when the outcome may not be positive for the company for reasons that are completely out of your control.

When this is the case, keep the focus on your role in the project and the way you completed your task. Do not dwell on the company's problems. This is about you and the skills you have to offer. Talk about what you were responsible for and how your part of the deal worked even if there were no positive results. An example would be a project that was shelved after you did all the work to complete it. That was out of your control.

How Long Should a Story Be?

When answering an interview question, it is best to be as focused as possible so that you can be succinct and to the point in as little time as possible: two minutes, more or less. When you ramble and bring in details that are not relevant to the question, you lose your audience, who in this case is your interviewer.

A successful answer to an interview question is one that addresses the question asked and gets to the point while not rambling. Here are two examples of answers to the same question. Note how one question addresses the question, and one rambles on and is not specific.

Question: "Can you give me an example of a time when you worked on a project that required a great deal of written communication?"

Rambling Example:

I've always been a good writer. My writing skills have always been my strong point. I have been commended on my writing ability in every performance review that I have ever had. I am very good at researching facts and following through on leads. In my last job, I was involved in the creation of our website by writing the content. That was a great experience. Working closely with the designers, I was able to contribute and add to the message that they were trying to get across. Writing isn't the major focus of my job responsibilities, but I do like to write very much. I have written some proposals, and they have been received very well. When I do have writing assignments, it is usually in addition to my regular job. I can tell you that whenever I have had the opportunity to write, I have received several comments on what a good job I have done. In fact, I was given an award for my writing skills as a team member on a project that received a grant. I am looking at this job as a chance to learn and develop my writing skills.

The listener (interviewer) hears that you have strong writing skills, but he probably had that idea after the first two lines. But you kept belaboring the point and adding irrelevant facts.

A Concise Two-minute Example
Problem:

That would be when I took over the responsibility of writing the department newsletter. This was my first experience at coordinating a publication from start to finish by myself.

Action:

The first thing I did was to consult with the people in the company that had written similar newsletters. This gave me a sense of what to do and what not to do. Next, I did an informal survey of company employees, everyone from the support staff to the director of the department. From their comments I came up with a new idea of getting the people involved. Each month I hold a writing contest and then publish the winners' stories. The employee involvement has made a big difference in my efforts.

Result:

Recently, the newsletter was awarded "most creative departmental newsletter." I was rewarded by my boss and the company.

You can see that the first question does not address the question asked and has irrelevant information in the answer, while the second answer gives a specific example of a time when you had a writing experience, which is what the question asked for.

A tip in interviewing is to take time to listen to the question. Next, take time to process how you are going to answer. Pre interview preparation will make a significant difference in your interview performance.

When you think about it, two minutes is a fair amount of time for a person to give his full attention to what others have to say. By sticking with the two-minute rule you will find that you will keep your interviewer interested and listening to your answer.

Your Inventory of Stories

The next step in your preparation process is to build an inventory of your stories so that you can pull from them when a question is asked that calls for a story. You will find this much easier than making up a story on the spot. Building your inventory will be covered in Chapter 7.

Situational/Hypothetical Questions

There is a huge difference between behavioral interviewing question and the situational or hypothetical question. Behavioral interviewing is about the past, while hypothetical questions are about the "future." The hypothetical question is about something that hasn't happened yet, but what if it did happen? What would you do?

A situational question example would be:

"What would you do if you encountered a problem?"

The problems can range from very specific to very general. What the interviewer is seeking in the situational/hypothetical question is a chance to see how you "think" through a problem. For example,

"What would you do if you had a problem with a fellow employee?"

The word *if* is the clue that the interviewer wants to hear about your thought process. This question does *not* require a past experience example. It is literally impossible to prepare for a specific situational question unless you have been given samples or information before the interview. A problem with a coworker could range from a conflict to an emergency situation and everything in between.

Once again, the use of factors will assist you in thinking through what the interviewer is seeking when he or she asks this type of question.

Here are some examples of situational questions and possible factors:

Question: "What would you do if you worked with a coworker whose negative attitude was affecting morale?"

(Possible factors: communication; motivation; relating with others; initiative)

Question: "You witness a coworker doing something illegal or against policy. What would you do?"

(Possible factors: integrity; honesty; decision making; communication)

Question: "You are asked to do something that will be unfair to your other coworkers but will result in a promotion for you. What would you do?"

(Possible factors: honesty; integrity; communication; team player)

Rather than try to out guess the interviewer, it is best to focus on the factor that is involved and then focus on your thinking process. Think about how you think through problems. When faced with certain problems, you probably have a natural way of handling them, a method that is your way of thinking.

A technique that has helped my clients to answer hypothetical or situational questions is to use a template to follow. You can use the template as a guide to think through the answer to the questions that ask, "What would do?" When you hear: "What would you do if ...," think of the ARDIE template.

The ARDIE Template

This example of a template is called ARDIE (Analyze, Research, Develop, Implement, Evaluate, and Reevaluate). Behind each letter, or word, there is a series of actions to think about as you relate your answer and show the interviewer how you think through a problem.

A: *The first thing I would do is to* **analyze**: *gathering information; evaluate; process and practices; customer or employee needs; business needs; desired business outcomes.*

R: *Next, I would do* **research**: *check additional facts: What has happened in the past?*

D: *Then I would* **develop**: *develop the overall plan; action steps.*

I: *After that I would* **implement**: *put the plan in place.*

E: *I always* **evaluate and reevaluate**: *monitor the outcomes; desired behaviors; business metrics; satisfaction.*

The idea of the template is to focus, and once again use your five fingers to remember the steps you want to follow. Sometimes it is easier to answer this type of question if you keep in mind a time when something like this actually happened. You can refer to a time when you handled a similar situation without giving the details of the situation. In other words, you would take a behavioral story step-by-step, without any details.

An example:

The first thing that I would do is to evaluate all the facts. I would do this by...

The next thing that I would do is to explore further and do research. I would do this by...

My next step would be to prepare a plan. The way I usually do this is to use a spreadsheet...

I would then put my plan into action. I would implement the plan by making sure...

Finally, I would follow through and reevaluate to make sure that this was going to solve the problem.

This is a good way to answer a situational question using the template. The biggest problem with answering this type of hypothetical question is not giving enough detail. One way to deal with this problem is to think through the processes you've used in the past to solve problems, and then walk through that process with lots of examples and details. It's a bit like telling a story, but it's more of a tale that you can spin any way you please.

Using The Template

A favorite example of a situational question was one that has been around for a while:

Question: What if you were the owner of a business that manufactured tennis balls, and the government outlawed the game of tennis in the United States. What would you do?

The question is a silly one, but one that can still be answered in a serious manner using the ARDIE template.

Answer:

A: *The first thing that I would do is to do an analysis of my inventory and my machinery. What options are available given what I have to work with?*

R: *Once I had that data, I would begin to research based on my info. I would contact other countries whose country still allowed the game to be played. I would also look into the cost of redesigning my current machinery to manufacture other sized balls. I would meet with my engineering staff to begin to think out of the box for ideas regarding new products that could use tennis balls.*

D: *I would then develop a plan, including the marketing of any new products and costs involved.*

I: *The implementation of the plan would be according to the seasonal needs for any products developed. We would roll out the product as quickly as possible.*

E: *I am a believer in follow-up and customer feedback. Based on any input we received, I would evaluate and make sure that the suggestions are taken seriously and changes made accordingly. I would continue this follow up, and reevaluate until there was a high percentage of customer satisfaction.*

The template may not work every time, but it can be the basis of thinking through the answer to many situational questions. Because these questions can be very slippery to answer, remember it's about the way you process and think through a problem that's important.

CHAPTER 7

Building Your Inventory: Preparing Your Stories

n Chapter 1, we covered how proper preparation prevents poor performance. This chapter will focus on preparing for your interview by writing out your stories and examples to prevent being caught off guard.

From a Client:

For me, writing out the stories was key. When I talk about myself, I don't usually focus on I did this, or I did that because that's not the interesting part of the story for me.

Forcing myself to write out the story in this format brought the things I did to the forefront. If I told the same story to a stranger, it wouldn't be as interesting, or the person I was talking to would probably think I had a huge ego. But in an artificial situation like the job interview, using this format was essential.

By having *an inventory of stories* to pull from, you will be able to adjust your stories to fit the situation or factor. Organizing your inventory of stories by factor will not only give you a resource of stories but a method to address what the interviewer is seeking as a key factor. You will be able to stop worrying about the questions and focus on the factors that the interviewer will be focusing on.

Example:

Question: "Tell me about a time when you had a conflict with a coworker."

By thinking "factor," you know that the interviewer is seeking examples of your ability to communicate and relate with others. But, what if you don't have a story ready that covers a conflict with a coworker?

One method I teach my clients is to try "morphing," or "putting a spin" on the answer.

(The words *morphing* or *morphed* serve as a means to communicate the idea of replacing one item for another. The meaning according to dictionary.com: "to transform or be transformed completely in appearance or character: he morphed from nerd into pop icon." In this case, we are using the term to change the original question to fit an answer you have, even though it's not a perfect match.)

Morphed Answer: "I have an example of a time when I had a conflict with my boss."

The factor is the same (communication and relating to others), and most of the time this method of morphing will give the interviewer the information needed. So, if the interviewer is focusing on the factor and how you communicate and relate with others, the morphed answer would show your ability in this area.

There will also be times when you do not have the work experience to answer this type of question, such as the person who is changing fields, re entering the workforce, or is a new student. If you don't have an example of a conflict with a coworker, you can use a life experience.

A Volunteer Job Example

Problem:

This is an example of how I handled a conflict in my volunteer job as a youth soccer referee. I had a conflict with one of the team coaches. He was being very disruptive and yelling after every call I made. This was extremely upsetting to not only me, but to the players and coaches of the other team as well.

Action:

What I did was, I walked over to the sideline and talked to this coach. He was talking down to me, saying how horrible the calls were and accusing me of favoring the other team. I told him he must control himself or I would have to kick him out of the park. The coach realized that I wasn't going to take his nonsense, and he walked back to the sidelines. Feeling that I got through to the coach by talking to him, I continued the game. Not too long after that I heard the coach yelling at my calls again. The next time the ball went out of bounds, I went back over to the sideline and told the coach in a stern voice, "Coach, I just spoke to you about your language. This is your last warning, and if I need to speak to you again during this game you will be thrown out." The coach realized that I was fed up with his tactics.

Result:

I didn't hear from the coach for the rest of the game. The two teams went on and finished the game, and after the game the coach ran over to me and apologized for his behavior. He said he got carried away and was sorry for causing the disturbance. The other coaches thanked me and told me I had handled the situation very professionally.

This is a very good example of "morphing" the story and still getting your point across.

The interviewer can hear that you were firm but professional. You were able to demonstrate that you can handle a difficult problem without losing your temper. The interviewer sees you in another setting, using your leadership skills, and you answered the question by morphing the answer.

If, for some reason, you run into a situation where there is resistance by the interviewer who wants an exact example to answer the question, you will have to dig deep and come up with an example of you and a coworker having a difference of opinion. Although this more than likely will not happen, it is always a good idea to be prepared for the unexpected.

Using Key Factors to Write Your Inventory of Stories

An inventory is a supply of things that you may need. An inventory of stories is a "stockpile" of information that you will use as needed to answer any questions that could arise. This is different from memorizing answers to questions that may not be asked. This is an inventory of stories based on factors that you have identified as relevant to this job. Your stories are interchangeable because they will cover more than one factor.

One of my clients wrote:

> This may sound ridiculous, but at times I was not even sure what question I was answering because I was focused on the factor.

Example: The Double Meaning Factors

Sometimes, a question may seem confusing because it could be the same factor only asked with a completely different slant. Below is an example of a double meaning of a factor.

Factor: communication; relating to others; convincing others.

There is a big difference between the following two questions:

"Tell me about a time when you had a conflict or difference of opinion with someone."

"Give me an example of a time when you convinced someone to change things your way."

Both questions relate to the factors of communication and relating to others, but there are two distinctly different skills that are being sought. What does it take to have good communication skills? You may think it's talking to others, and that would be correct. But communication goes beyond just talking. It means being able to handle yourself in situations in which you relate to others, sometimes under stress. The greater majority of jobs require good communication skills, whether it's relating to people who have problems, convincing others to do things your way, or giving lectures in front of groups.

This is where you will begin to read between the lines. For example, if you are going to apply for a sales position, communication will be quite different than if you are applying for a position as a scientist. The salesperson will need good customer service skills with an ability to convince others that whatever he is selling is going to make a difference in the customer's life. Whereas the scientist will require good communication skills in order to communicate in a report, request a grant, or present to fellow colleagues or members of the community. These are two different methods of relating to others, but both fall under the factor "communication and relating to others."

Because of the overlap between some of the factors, plus the double meaning that some factors can have, it is suggested that you think of two examples for each factor. It is always good to have a backup story when you are pulling from your reserve.

Writing Your Stories

When you first start writing your stories, it will be easier if you focus on one factor per story, even though the story may involve multiple factors. Think of it like learning to play golf.

The first thing you need to learn is to hit the ball. Later, as you improve, you can learn the more difficult shots. Right now, aim for the factor.

RULE OF THUMB

Proportions of a story are as important as the story itself.

Using the most common factors as a base, it is suggested that you begin to build your inventory of stories around these factors. Once you have an actual job description or posting to work from, you can refine the list to match the needs of the job.

Most Common Factors

The following brief list of factors is explained in in more detail in the previous section.

- Honesty and integrity: moral issues
- Communication: relating to others, convincing others
- Adaptable: open to change, flexible
- Problem solving: analyze, evaluate, judgments/decisions
- Initiative: above and beyond, resourceful
- Leadership: motivate, role model, team player
- Plan and organize: prioritize
- Accountable: results-oriented
- Composure: to stay positive calm under pressure
- Self-motivated: enthusiastic, passionate

EXERCISE

Your Stories: Building Your Inventory

By using this template with each of your stories and then checking the proportions of the story, you will begin to become more confident about writing your examples. You will begin to be a good storyteller.

Key Factor: Honesty and Integrity

Problem (20 Percent of Story), Five to Seven Sentences

(Write the beginning of your story)

Action (60 Percent of the Story), Seven to Nine Steps, More or Less

(Use this phrase to signal to the interviewer, and to yourself, that the plot of the story is beginning.)

Use the phrases, "What I did was..." or "The first step I took was..."—whatever phrase works for you to signal action.

(Steps taken...)

Result (20 Percent of the Story), Three to Five Sentences

(Remember to add third-party endorsement, if appropriate.)

Check the proportions

- Does your story have a clear beginning (20 percent)?
- Is it clear where you are and what your role is?
- Is there an introduction to announce the action?
- Does the action include "showing," or is it mostly "telling"? Is it 60 percent?
- Is there a clear ending to your story? Is it 20 percent?
- Are there any kudos, rewards, or third-party endorsements?

Key Factor: Communication: Relating to Others

Problem (20 Percent of Story), Five to Seven Sentences

(Write the beginning of your story.)

Action (60 Percent of the Story), Seven to Nine Steps, More or Less

(Use this phrase to signal to the interviewer, and to yourself, that the plot of the story is beginning.)

Use the phrases, "What I did was…" or "The first step I took was…"—whatever phrase works for you to signal action.

(Steps taken…)

Result (20 Percent of the Story), Three to Five Sentences

(Remember to add third-party endorsement, if appropriate.)

Check the proportions

- Does your story have a clear beginning (20 percent)?

- Is it clear where you are and what your role is?

- Is there an introduction to announce the action?

- Does the action include "showing," or is it mostly "telling"? Is it 60 percent?

- Is there a clear ending to your story? Is it 20 percent?

- Are there any kudos, rewards, or third-party endorsements?

Key Factor: Adaptable, Open to Change, Flexible

Problem (20 Percent of Story), Five to Seven Sentences

(Write the beginning of your story.)

Action (60 Percent of the Story), Seven to Nine Steps, More or Less

(Use this phrase to signal to the interviewer, and to yourself, that the plot of the story is beginning.)

Use the phrases, "What I did was..." or "The first step I took was..."—whatever phrase works for you to signal action.

(Steps taken...)

Result (20 Percent of the Story), Three to Five Sentences

(Remember to add third-party endorsement, if appropriate.)

Check the proportions

- Does your story have a clear beginning (20 percent)?
- Is it clear where you are and what your role is?
- Is there an introduction to announce the action?
- Does the action include "showing," or is it mostly "telling"? Is it 60 percent?
- Is there a clear ending to your story? Is it 20 percent?
- Are there any kudos, rewards, or third-party endorsements?

Key Factor: Problem Solving: Analyze, Evaluate, Judgments/Decisions

Problem (20 Percent of Story), Five to Seven Sentences

(Write the beginning of your story.)

Action (60 Percent of the Story), Seven to Nine Steps, More or Less

(Use this phrase to signal to the interviewer, and to yourself, that the plot of the story is beginning.)

Use the phrases, "What I did was…" or "The first step I took was…"—whatever phrase works for you to signal action.

(Steps taken…)

Result (20 Percent of the Story), Three to Five Sentences

(Remember to add third-party endorsement, if appropriate.)

Check the proportions

- Does your story have a clear beginning (20 percent)?
- Is it clear where you are and what your role is?
- Is there an introduction to announce the action?
- Does the action include "showing," or is it mostly "telling"? Is it 60 percent?
- Is there a clear ending to your story? Is it 20 percent?
- Are there any kudos, rewards, or third-party endorsements?

Key Factor: Initiative: Above and Beyond, Resourceful

Problem (20 Percent of Story), Five to Seven Sentences

(Write the beginning of your story.)

Action (60 Percent of the Story), Seven to Nine Steps, More or Less

(Use this phrase to signal to the interviewer, and to yourself, that the plot of the story is beginning.)

Use the phrases, "What I did was..." or "The first step I took was..."—whatever phrase works for you to signal action.

(Steps taken...)

Result (20 Percent of the Story), Three to Five Sentences

(Remember to add third-party endorsement, if appropriate.)

Check the proportions

- Does your story have a clear beginning (20 percent)?
- Is it clear where you are and what your role is?
- Is there an introduction to announce the action?
- Does the action include "showing," or is it mostly "telling"? Is it 60 percent?
- Is there a clear ending to your story? Is it 20 percent?
- Are there any kudos, rewards, or third-party endorsements?

Key Factor: Leadership: Motivate, Role Model, Team Player

Problem (20 Percent of Story), Five to Seven Sentences

(Write the beginning of your story.)

Action (60 Percent of the Story), Seven to Nine Steps, More or Less

(Use this phrase to signal to the interviewer, and to yourself, that the plot of the story is beginning.)

Use the phrases, "What I did was..." or "The first step I took was..."—whatever phrase works for you to signal action.

(Steps taken...)

Result (20 Percent of the Story), Three to Five Sentences

(Remember to add third-party endorsement, if appropriate.)

Check the proportions

- Does your story have a clear beginning (20 percent)?
- Is it clear where you are and what your role is?
- Is there an introduction to announce the action?
- Does the action include "showing," or is it mostly "telling"? Is it 60 percent?
- Is there a clear ending to your story? Is it 20 percent?
- Are there any kudos, rewards, or third-party endorsements?

Key Factor: Plan and Organize: Prioritize

Problem (20 Percent of Story), Five to Seven Sentences

(Write the beginning of your story.)

Action (60 Percent of the Story), Seven to Nine Steps, More or Less

(Use this phrase to signal to the interviewer, and to yourself, that the plot of the story is beginning.)

Use the phrases, "What I did was..." or "The first step I took was..."—whatever phrase works for you to signal action.

(Steps taken...)

Result (20 Percent of the Story), Three to Five Sentences

(Remember to add third-party endorsement, if appropriate.)

Check the proportions

- Does your story have a clear beginning (20 percent)?
- Is it clear where you are and what your role is?
- Is there an introduction to announce the action?
- Does the action include "showing," or is it mostly "telling"? Is it 60 percent?
- Is there a clear ending to your story? Is it 20 percent?
- Are there any kudos, rewards, or third-party endorsements?

Key Factor: Accountable: Results-Oriented

Problem (20 Percent of Story), Five to Seven Sentences

(Write the beginning of your story.)

Action (60 Percent of the Story), Seven to Nine Steps, More or Less

(Use this phrase to signal to the interviewer, and to yourself, that the plot of the story is beginning.)

Use the phrases, "What I did was…" or "The first step I took was…"—whatever phrase works for you to signal action.

(Steps taken…)

Result (20 Percent of the Story), Three to Five Sentences

(Remember to add third-party endorsement, if appropriate.)

Check the proportions

- Does your story have a clear beginning (20 percent)?
- Is it clear where you are and what your role is?
- Is there an introduction to announce the action?
- Does the action include "showing," or is it mostly "telling"? Is it 60 percent?
- Is there a clear ending to your story? Is it 20 percent?
- Are there any kudos, rewards, or third-party endorsements?

Key factor: composure: to stay positive, calm under pressure

Problem (20 Percent of Story), Five to Seven Sentences

(Write the beginning of your story.)

Action (60 Percent of the Story), Seven to Nine Steps, More or Less

(Use this phrase to signal to the interviewer, and to yourself, that the plot of the story is beginning.)

Use the phrases, "What I did was…" or "The first step I took was…"—whatever phrase works for you to signal action.

(Steps taken…)

Result (20 Percent of the Story), Three to Five Sentences

(Remember to add third-party endorsement, if appropriate.)

Check the proportions

- Does your story have a clear beginning (20 percent)?

- Is it clear where you are and what your role is?

- Is there an introduction to announce the action?

- Does the action include "showing," or is it mostly "telling"? Is it 60 percent?

- Is there a clear ending to your story? Is it 20 percent?

- Are there any kudos, rewards, or third-party endorsements?

Key Factor: Self-Motivated: Enthusiastic, Passionate

Problem (20 Percent of Story), Five to Seven Sentences

(Write the beginning of your story.)

Action (60 Percent of the Story), Seven to Nine Steps, More or Less

(Use this phrase to signal to the interviewer, and to yourself, that the plot of the story is beginning.)

Use the phrases, "What I did was…" or "The first step I took was…"— whatever phrase works for you to signal action.

(Steps taken…)

Result (20 Percent of the Story), Three to Five Sentences

(Remember to add third-party endorsement, if appropriate.)

Check the proportions

- Does your story have a clear beginning (20 percent)?

- Is it clear where you are and what your role is?

- Is there an introduction to announce the action?

- Does the action include "showing," or is it mostly "telling"? Is it 60 percent?

- Is there a clear ending to your story? Is it 20 percent?

- Are there any kudos, rewards, or third-party endorsements?

The Backup Plan

Remember, it is best if you have a reserve story to use for each factor, just in case. Writing your inventory of stories may seem like a tedious task, but it is work that will pay off when you sit in the interview and have your stories prepared and ready to answer those difficult questions. It will be much easier preparing the stories before the interview than coming up with stories on the spot during the interview. The feeling of being prepared will boost your confidence and, as a result, affect your performance during the interview.

Organize Your Factors

Words of wisdom from a client:

> When a question was asked me in the interview, my
> brain snapped right to the factor. Since I had catego-
> rized my stories by factor, I was able to scroll down a
> list in my brain of which story to choose. This gave me
> tremendous latitude to select which story to tell, much
> like I was browsing a shelf of DVDs deciding which
> movie to watch.

There are many ways you can organize your inventory of
stories so that you will be able to pull one up just by thinking
of the factor. Another way to think of organizing your stories
is to think of a file drawer with Pendaflex files. Each tab will
represent a factor, and within the files are your stories.

There is no one that knows your stories better than you,
so if you forget a fact or a word, it really won't matter as long as
you get your point across through your example. Don't try to
memorize your stories, but know the points and proportions of
the story well enough to be a good storyteller.

CHAPTER 8

The Five Categories of Interview Questions

The intent of this book is to teach you techniques to deal with interview questions by thinking about what's behind the question, not memorizing answers. There will be a number of questions that may be asked in the interview that you should be prepared to answer. By classifying these questions into five categories you will have an idea of how to use the information that has been covered in the previous parts of this book.

Category One: Who Are You and What Do You Have to Offer?

Below are examples of questions that all fall under the same category of "Getting to know you." The one thing that all of these questions have in common is that they are focused on getting to know you, what you can do, and the questions "Tell me about yourself," and "What do you have to offer?" By preparing your five points (Chapter 5) you will be able to answer most of these questions using some, or all of the points.

- **Tell me about yourself.** What's behind this question? This is another way of asking, "Who are you?" Where you focus your statement will be the most important part of this answer. You can use the identified factors from the job posting to emphasize your fit to the position in addition to using the Five Points. You can use the points as you have written them, or perhaps emphasize one point over another. For example, say something like, "I am an energetic person who knows how to get things done. In my five years working experience I have..." The Five Points don't always have to be cited in the exact order as you wrote them; just adjust your "five-finger memory tool" so that you can remember them step-by-step.

- **Why should I hire you?** What's behind this question? The interviewer is basically saying, "Sell me. Why should I buy?" Any salesperson will tell you that in order to sell someone something, you must first deal with the customer's (in this case the interviewer's) needs. By comparing these needs with your qualifications, you will be able to answer the question asked on the basis of what the job requires. To answer this question, you can use your Five Points to summarize what you have to offer, especially for any questions asking, "Who are you?" Keeping your preparation focused and simplifying what you want the interviewer to know about you will take some of the fear out of the interview process. You will feel prepared and more confident.

- **Why do you feel you are qualified for this position?**
  What's behind this question? This is an aggressive
  question that basically asks, "What can you offer this
  company? This is not a place for self-doubt with answers
  like, "I think I can," or "I'm pretty sure I can." A confident
  answer is called for, such as, "I am very qualified for this
  job. I have looked over the job posting and what is needed
  to fill this position, and I know that I have what you're
  looking for." Once again, by summarizing the Five Points
  you've written plus identifying the factors, your skills,
  abilities, and traits, you will be prepared to answer this
  question. Your preparation steps will begin to pay off.

- **How can you bring added value to the company?**
  What's behind this question? This is the same question
  as, "How can you make a difference working here?"
  The interviewer is asking you to tell him what you can
  do to make his life easier and more successful, if he is
  the hiring manager. He is interested in hearing about
  your added value and past successes. The answer to this
  question is answered by talking about your expertise
  through your experiences and your accomplishments. If
  you've done your homework and compared what they are
  seeking against what you have to offer, you can determine
  where you are strongest and tell the interviewer. Any
  time you have "added value" to bring to a company,
  whether through languages, people skills, or the ability
  to do something that most candidates cannot, you should
  sell the value as a strong point. Depending on how
  important your value is to the position, this could make
  the difference in your being the chosen candidate.

- **Why should we hire you over the other candidates?**
  What's behind this question? The interviewer is trying
  to decide which candidate to choose. This is a chance
  for you to talk about your expertise, accomplishments,
  and any other extra skills you have. For instance, you
  may be an accountant with an engineering degree.
  Or, you may speak another language that is not
  required for the job, but would be useful for working
  with diverse customers. Your Five Points can guide
  you through your area of expertise and your strengths.
  Remember, to ask yourself, "What's important to this
  interviewer?"

- **What makes you the best candidate for this job?**
  What's behind this question? As in the previous
  questions, the interviewer is asking for help deciding
  which candidate to choose. This is not a time for
  modesty. Do you believe in yourself? If so, convince
  the interviewer that you are the best because of what
  you bring. A quick summary of your Five Points will
  add weight to your answer and make it stronger. And,
  don't rule out the "likeability" factor. Be yourself,
  and let the interviewer get to know the real you. You
  might say something like, "Anyone who has worked
  with me in the past would tell you that you would be
  making the best decision by hiring me because of my
  contagious energy and positive attitude."

You can probably come up with more examples of questions that fit this category from questions you were asked in
your own interview experiences. The information to answer

these basic questions was covered in Chapter 2 and Chapter 5. Doing your homework and being prepared will enable you to answer most of the questions in this category. The basic premise to remember about this category is that your total package is who you are and what you bring to the position.

Question: "Why should we hire you?"

Answers that *won't work*:

Because I need a job.

This answer is about you. Employers want to know what you can do for "them."

I am a hard worker.

This is a really trite answer. Almost anyone can say he or she is a hard worker.

I saw your ad and knew I could do the job.

This answer lacks passion and purpose. It says, "I'll take anything that is out there."

Stronger answers that would get the interviewer's attention:

Because I have three years' work experience, working with customers in a very similar environment. I know what to expect in this position.

Because I have what it takes to fill the requirements of this job: namely, deal with customers' problems using my developed customer service skills.

Because I have the experience and expertise in the area of customer support that is required in this position, and I really enjoy doing this job.

Category Two: Why Do You Want to Work Here?

Telling the interviewer why you want to work at the company is a very important question, and how you answer it could make or break the interview. The interviewer is testing you to see if you really want to work for *this* company, in *this* particular job. This is a broad question that can take you down the wrong path unless you have done some thinking about what to say ahead of time. Below is a list of questions that the interviewer might ask to reveal your intentions or goals.

- **Why are you leaving your current position?** What's behind this question?) The question is very reasonable. "Why are you available?" The concern is whether something negative happened to make you decide to leave your current job. Do you have a good reason for quitting your company other than you wanted a "challenge"? Your answer to this question should be prepared before the interview and should describe your situation in as positive a manner as possible. (The "seeking a challenge" answer is very overused and tired. Not a good answer by itself.)

RULE OF THUMB

Never tell a lie in an interview. If it eventually catches up with you, the only way out is to tell another lie. This is a good way to find yourself out of a job if the lie is ever discovered once you've been hired.

- **Why did you leave your last position?** What's behind this question?) The interviewer wants to know what happened. Did you get laid off or did you quit? In the event that there were unpleasant circumstances when you left your last job, this is not a good time to deal with any negative feelings you have. Being honest and forthright, but at the same time staying positive about your situation is the best way to handle this question. A good example would be:

There were six rounds of layoffs at my last company. I survived five rounds, but when it came to round six they had to cut deep. My position was eliminated along with half of my group because the project we were working on was cancelled.

Not everyone will have such a definite statement to make, but whatever your situation, it is very helpful if you script an answer ahead of time so that you won't dread this question. The most important thing is to "keep it simple." No need to add a ton of information that is not of interest to your interviewer. Basically, the interviewer wants to know if you are going to be a problem employee.

- **What are you looking for in your next position?** What's behind this question? The interviewer is trying to find out if this job will satisfy you. How long will you stick around? Are you taking this job as a stepping-stone? This is a good time to talk about your goals, provided you have career goals. Be as specific as possible while not eliminating yourself from the running by being too specific. For example, you wouldn't want to overstep with a goal that is probably not achievable at this company. It is a good idea to think of the steps you want to take if you are offered this job and beyond.

You might say that I am stepping back to go forward. I believe that it is easy to lose touch with the bigger picture, and I see this as an opportunity to do something different from what I have been doing. Long term I would like to assume more responsibility and move up in the organization if possible.

- **What are your expectations of this job?** What's behind this question? A win/win outcome is always desirable when hiring someone for a job. Is this the right candidate for the job? And, is this the right job for this candidate? The interviewer is asking you what you think it would be like to work in this job. If you have expectations that won't be met, the interviewer should let you know now. The hiring process is a costly endeavor, and avoiding bad hiring decisions is the intent of the interviewer. Be sure you have done your homework and have a good idea of what the company culture is, and in particular, what the job you're applying for entails. Using the shotgun approach and being willing to take any job may solve a temporary problem, but it is not a long-term solution.

- **What are your career objectives and goals?** What's behind this question? This is another question regarding your intent to stay with the company. Are you in it for the long haul, or is this just a quick fix to your current financial problem? Will you leave if a better opportunity comes along in the next few months or so? When discussing your goals, it is safest to break them down into short-term and long-term goals. Here is an example of a possible way to answer this question:

  I like to break down goals into short-term goals, with the long-term goals in mind. Right now, I'm looking for a position in a company with a solid track record. I want to contribute to a team, bringing my extensive experience in this field to add to the team mix. Long-term goals will depend on the career path available at the company. Ideally, I would like to move progressively within a company.

  If this answer sounds too canned or formal to you, try a different technique. Think of how you would present the answer if you were talking to a colleague about your situation. What details would you share with him or her?

- **Where do you see this role going?** What's behind this question? This is an open-ended question that is similar to, "Where do you see yourself in five years?" This type of question can throw most candidates off balance. If you're the type of person who prefers an organized way of life, you may find this question to be a "piece of cake." You like to plan ahead, and have a plan that you want to follow. But, if you are among the majority of persons who let life happen as it comes along, you will probably not have a smooth answer without some forethought. In the fast-paced world we live in, it is difficult for anyone to predict what he or she will be doing five to ten years from now. Your answer should be sincere but an answer that is not necessarily "set in stone."

- **What is there about this opportunity that most excites you?** What's behind this question? The best answer will come from you thinking about what you want. If this is a job you really want, then let your enthusiasm show, or as some people like to say, "Show your passion."

Here is an example of an enthusiastic answer:

I found the job posting on the Internet, and I have to admit I hadn't heard of your company. But once I started doing my research I was very impressed with what I saw and the direction that your company is moving. As I went through the requirements of this job and matched them against my experience and skills, it just started to click into place. I believe I am a perfect match for this position. I have a great deal of experience doing this type of job, and your company values are in line with the values I am seeking in a job.

No one can tell you exactly how to answer this type of question. It will come from what is important to you. However, the more focused and employer-centered you can be about your goal, the better your chances will be of steering the interview in the right direction.

Category Three: Sensitive or Negative Questions

As you've prepared for the interview you've spent your time preparing answers to "positive questions." You've been working on demonstrating how good you are and what you can offer this position. What you probably have not prepared is answers to questions regarding your weaknesses and failures—the times when you were challenged by difficult situations. So what do you do when you encounter a "curveball?" The answer is you deal with it in a positive manner.

Turning negatives into positives is an important skill to learn. When you are asked a "bad" or negative question, take a minute to turn the answer around, refocusing the answer to include some positive qualities. Below are some negative questions that you could be asked in an interview that are more than likely the questions you dread most.

- **What is your weakness?** The most dreaded question of all. Who wants to admit to weaknesses? This is especially true in an interview. One way to handle this question is by minimizing the weakness and emphasizing the strengths. Stay away from personal qualities, (i.e., "I'm shy") and concentrate on professional traits. One formula for this type of questions has been around for a while. It's called "The Sandwich Technique." The formula starts with a "positive," then slips in the "negative," and ends with an action that you are working on to change the situation (a positive). Of course, you would only say you are working on changing something negative if it is true.

Positive, Negative, Positive Formula

- (+) Begin with a positive statement
- (–) Slip in the negative (or weakness)
- (+) End with a positive statement

Example

I consider myself to be a good presenter, and I get positive feedback when I present. But I am always working on improving my communication skills to be a more effective presenter. I take every opportunity to practice speaking before groups. I have also joined Toastmasters to improve my skills.

- **Tell me something negative about yourself.** This is another question that you'd probably rather not deal with in an interview. It's basically the same question that asks about your weaknesses. Since no person is perfect, we are all in need of improvement somewhere. Is there a particular area where you are trying to improve? This should be work-related, if possible. Perhaps it's learning a new skill, or improving on a skill that could be stronger with some practice or education. It could also be learning to be more tolerant of various people. The main thing is that it should be a realistic goal that you are working on changing. If you're a quiet, reserved person, it is unlikely that you will suddenly change into an outgoing, opinionated person overnight. Also, be wary of saying anything that might be an important factor to perform in this job. For example, if the job posting calls for well-developed computer skills and you are weak in this area, it is probably not a good idea to point this out as your weakness. Some people like to say that they are working on their communication skills. Since communication is one of the key factors that most employers look for in an employee, this is probably not the best thing to say.

- **What would your last boss tell me if I asked her what you needed to improve on?** This could be a ticklish question if you and your last boss did not hit it off. In fact, for some candidates, this just happens to be the very reason they're leaving their current job. If your last boss doesn't work as a good answer, try telling them about a boss that you did get along with.

I had an especially good relationship with my boss at my job at XYZ Company. What she would tell you

*is that I was her "right hand man," and more. She'd
probably tell you to expect me to be a nag if you need
to be reminded of your schedule or tasks. We used to
laugh about that fact.*

If the interviewer pushes for your last boss's comments,
explain that you and he had very different styles and never
achieved the same relationship you had with your previous boss. Of course, your individual circumstances will dic-
tate how you answer this question. But, if possible try to
keep it positive without "bad-mouthing" anyone. It's a small
world, and we never know who knows whom in the world
of work.

- **Have you ever been fired?** The interviewer is
  trying to find out about the "skeletons" in your
  closet. If you happened to have been fired, it is best
  to deal with any negative feeling you have about the
  situation before you get to the interview. The fact is
  people get fired every day. They move on and get
  new jobs. No matter what the circumstances, it is
  best to put it behind you. Deal with your feelings
  about the firing before the interview by scripting
  a statement that you feel comfortable about. An
  example would be:

*Yes. I was fired when I made a mistake in judgment
that went against company policy. I'm not proud
of what I did and was hard on myself about the*

mistake, but I also learned a great deal from the incident. There is no point holding on to the past. I will be more careful about my actions in the future. I am ready for a second chance and know that I will be a better employee because of this experience.

It is important that you display confidence and not get emotional when you talk about this incident. Remember, no one is perfect, and we all make mistakes.

- **What did you like least about your previous job and company?** This is another question in which the interviewer is seeking information about your motivation and what you don't like. What part of this job would you rather not do? It is best if you can keep it positive, and by all means, be sure to stay away from duties that are a part of the job you are interviewing for. As an example, if the job posting states that there is 25 percent travel, it could be a disaster if you were to tell the interviewer what you liked least about your last job was all the travel involved. Not a good idea.

- **Tell me about a time you worked (or led) a team and the effort failed.** What's behind this question? First of all, this is a behavioral question and it is asking for an example or a story. The interviewer wants to know how you work with teams, and when the team fails, how you react. Do you hold a grudge, or are you reasonable about your reaction to failure? Remember, this is a time to describe "your role" on the team and whether you could have done anything about the failure. Did your part of the project succeed, or were you a part of the failure? You may not have had anything to do with the failure and the result was out of your hands, and you completed your part of the project. If there is a "third-party" endorsement telling you that you did a good job of handling your part even though the team failed, it would be great to use the quote to convince the interviewer that you know how to handle team failure without blaming and holding a grudge.

- **Why have you had so many jobs over the past few years?** What's behind this question? If this question pertains to your situation, you'd probably rather not talk about it in the interview. Whatever your situation, be brief. Most people tell so many details that the interviewer gets lost while listening. Going into an interview with baggage is like dragging a big black garbage bag along behind you and parking it next to your chair during the interview. Nobody wants to hear about your problems. Some people's lives begin to sound like a soap opera because there have been so many extenuating circumstances. Don't feel compelled to share every detail with the interviewer. Whatever your situation, deal with any negative feelings before going to the interview.

- **"Tell me about a time when you had to handle a stressful situation."** What's behind this question? The interviewer wants an example of how you behaved in a stressful situation. Can you handle stress? Are you calm in a crisis? Do you remain positive when things begin to fall apart? This is a "behavioral" interviewing question. The clue to behavioral questions are the words, "Tell me about a time…" or "Can you give me an example of a time…" These questions are best answered by a "story," with a beginning, a middle, and an end. The story begins by describing the situation and then moves into the action—what your role was in the example. As with any good story, there must be a conclusion or ending. Preparing your stories is an important step in improving your success rate. Behavioral stories are covered in Chapter 6.

Category Four: What Are Your Salary Expectations?

Chapter 4 of this book covered many of the rules of dealing with salary questions. Here are a few more sample questions and answers to assist you in formulating your own answers to questions about salary during the interview. Some of the answers are stronger than others, and some will fit certain situations better than others. You will want to use your own words to answer this type of question. However, these examples will provide words to use that may be more effective in answering these difficult questions.

Questions and Answers

Question: "What are your salary expectations?"

(A) *I was making $60,000 at my last job, plus bonuses. I would be expecting at least that and a 15 percent to 20 percent increase.*
(This is not a good answer.)

(B) *I'm sure whatever you offer will be a fair amount for a person with my qualifications. Salary is not the most important factor to me. I'm looking for opportunity.*
(This is a weak answer.)

(C) *I really need more information about the job before we start to discuss salary. I'd like to postpone that discussion until later. Maybe you could tell me what is budgeted for the position, and how your commission structure works.*
(This is the best answer.)

Question: "What do you expect in the way of salary?"

(A) *Before I answer that question, I'd like to ask what you typically pay someone with my experience and education in this type of position.*
(Good answer.)

(B) *I'm sure when the time comes and I know more about the facts of the position and how it fits into the bigger picture, we can come to a mutually agreeable figure.*
(Good answer.)

(C) *I really need more information about the position before I can begin to discuss salary. Can you tell me the range budgeted for this position?*
(Good answer.)

Question: "What salary are you/were you making at your last job?"

(A) *It would be very difficult for me to compare my last salary with this position for various reasons, primarily because I don't have enough information about your whole package. I'm sure we can discuss this subject and your entire package before an offer is made.*
(Good answer.)

(B) *That would be like comparing two jobs that are entirely different in responsibilities and in the base and bonus structure. I would be more interested in hearing what the package you offer is before I compare the two jobs. I hope we can postpone this subject until we both have more information to discuss salary and benefit comparisons.*
(Good answer.)

(C) *I had an unusual situation at my last job where I took less salary to own a share of the company. I also had a bonus structure that I was receiving. I would have to look at the entire package that you offer before comparing the two jobs or salaries.*
(Good answer.)

Question: "Would you consider taking less pay than you made in your last job?"

(A) *I would really need to know more about the opportunity and your whole package before I can give you an answer to that question. You may offer extra perks that my last job may not have had, or vice versa. Basically, I need more information before I can answer that.*
(Good answer.)

(B) *While my highest career value is not money, it is important to me that I be fairly compensated for the work I do. I would be willing to consider a fair offer based on what I bring to the position in the way of experience and education.*

(Good answer.)

(C) *Opportunity is valuable to me. I am always willing to look at the bigger picture. I would want to be paid according to what I bring to the position, but would be willing to be somewhat flexible.*

(Good answer.)

You will notice that most of these examples attempt to defer the subject until you have more information and a better idea of whether this is the right job for you. When you have that information, you will be able to assess whether this is a job where you have something to offer and what the value should be — in other words, what you deserve to be paid.

What is the lowest salary you are willing to accept (no matter how terrific the job)?

If you do some calculations and figure out what you want and what you need to maintain your current lifestyle or to improve your current lifestyle, you will know when you have to say, "No, I can't accept the offer at that salary."

Whether you negotiate a salary or not is secondary to doing your homework before accepting an offer. It is always best to take some time before signing on the dotted line so that you understand exactly what you are gaining or losing.

Category Five: Miscellaneous Questions

There is no way to predict what types of questions will be asked in any interview. Questions will vary according to the job, the industry, the location, and the level of responsibility. This last category will include possible questions that can come up in interviews.

Miscellaneous questions can range from asking for your opinion on a subject to asking obscure questions that have not been covered in this book.

Examples

- What do you think is the most pressing issue or challenge for our industry?
- Describe a book that you've read recently.
- How do you spend your spare time?
- How do you deal with stress?

You can't prepare for every question possible, all you can do is try to answer as clearly as possible using the tools covered in the previous chapters.

Your Turn to Ask Questions

At some point, usually at the conclusion of the interview, you may be asked, "Do you have any questions?" A common answer to this question is, "No, I think you've covered everything very well." This is the wrong answer! You have passed up your opportunity to ask some critical questions that may make a difference to whether you want to work for this company.

Timing is the key to asking appropriate questions. The first round of interviews is about discovery: finding out about the job and the company, not about the benefits or raises. Good questions to ask in the first round are about the job content, the company culture, and the future of the company.

Here are some suggestions of the types of questions that you could ask at various points in the interview:

1. **Ask questions about topics that came up during the interview.**

    What that means is if the interviewer talked a lot about a certain thing, for example "databases," make sure you ask some questions about databases. You could ask: "It seems from the questions you have asked me there is a great deal of... in this job. Could you tell me more about that?" Or, you could say: "From what I am picking up today, it seems like.... Is that correct?"

    Asking for more information about the job shows an interest on your part, and it also shows the interviewer that you have been listening—and reading between the lines. You can take some small notes during the interview to remember specific areas in which you would like clarification.

    "Do you have any doubts that I can do this job?"

    This question may feel too risky for some people to ask. But, if the interviewer has doubts, and he will tell you, there is always the chance that you can explain something that he may have missed during the interview:

The interviewer's concern: "I am concerned that you lack any experience supervising people."

Your reply: "As you may have seen on my résumé, I volunteer on a continual basis with Habitat for Humanity. I have supervised several projects involving a diverse group of people. I assign duties and schedules, as well as handle any personnel problems that come up. I'd be glad to give you examples if you'd like to hear them." By telling the interviewer that you have experience in another area, you may just be able to convince her that you are capable of doing what she is concerned about. It may not be what the interviewer wants to hear, but it is better than not giving vital information about your background.

2. **"Is there any additional information that I can provide to you that would convince you that I am the best person for this job ... (drum roll) because I believe I am."**

   (Say this only if you do believe you are.) This is kind of like "closing" or "asking for the sale." It is an extremely important step in any sales transaction, and you'd be surprised how many salespeople don't ask for the job at the end of the interview.

These answers can be used according to the situation and your interviewer. You will have to judge whether any of these questions are appropriate for you.

Questions *not* to ask in the first rounds of interviewing:

- Questions about salary, stock options, vacation, holiday schedule, benefits.
- Don't ask questions that have already been answered in the interview.
- Don't "grill" the interviewer; it's okay to ask about the person's background, but as an interested party, not an interrogator.

Questions TO ASK in the first rounds of interviewing:

- Ask for a copy of the job description.
- Why is this job open?
- What qualities are you seeking in the person for this job?
- What is the next step? When will you make your selection?

Keep Your Sunny Side Up

If you've been searching for a job for more than a few weeks or even months, you may be experiencing feelings of defeat and despair, not to mention the urge to give up. It's been a tough year, and then some, for those who have lost jobs for whatever reason. Interviewing with no second interviews or offers coming in begins to wear thin very fast.

Here are five rules to encourage optimism and discourage negativity:

1. **Accept that there will be ups and downs.**

   It's not unusual to have highs and lows during your job search. Some days you may even feel like you're on an emotional roller coaster. Everything looks hopeful one moment with a job prospect ahead, and then it changes to dark and dismal in the next moment when you receive a rejection. Accepting the fact that this is a stressful time you are going through and that a great deal of it is out of your control will help you put things into perspective.

2. **Give yourself permission to fail.**

   It is very disappointing when you feel like you "aced" the interview and then wait for the promised call that never comes. Be realistic; you aren't going to get a job offer after every interview. Think of it this way: you didn't marry every person you ever dated (at least most of us didn't), and you aren't going to get a job offer after every interview. And maybe that's a good thing, at least some of the time. Remember, you are interviewing "them" as much as they are interviewing you.

3. **Work on controlling stress.**

   Stress becomes a problem when it begins to affect your lifestyle and health. Are you waking up in the middle of the night or skipping meals because you are feeling really down or upset? You may need to talk to someone who is a professional to get some advice about relaxation techniques. Park and Recreation departments in most cities offer relaxation courses of some kind—yoga, Pilates, aerobics, or stress control exercises—for a nominal fee. Do whatever you can to work on getting yourself back on balance.

4. **Continue to get "out there."**

Study after study published continues to indicate that "networking" is still the number one way to land a job. Take advantage of every opportunity to be with groups of people. This encompasses everything from networking online to your child's soccer game. Informal networking can happen at any moment and when you least expect it. An example is of a man waiting for a bus. He struck up a conversation with another man also waiting for the bus and ended up getting a job lead and an eventual offer. No one can predict when an opportunity might come your way.

5. **Prepare yourself.**

Preparing ahead of the interview will give you a definite advantage. What this means is getting focused about what you want the interviewer to know about you. You are presenting a picture of you with words. It is important to identify what makes you unique and what added value you can bring to the position. Reading through the job posting you are applying for and getting a sense of what it will take to do this job will help you look at the process from an interviewer's point of view. You want to let the interviewer know that you are the "solution to the problem," and the best person for the job.

You are not alone. Remember that it is an *extremely* tight job market and that for every job opening there are four or five equally qualified candidates standing in line behind you. It is essential that you are prepared, focused, and able to tell the interviewer what makes you unique and why you are the best person for the job.

Keeping upbeat is a part of your job right now. When you begin to give in to the "dark side" you will project that to others. You want to stay as upbeat as possible, particularly while interviewing. Bringing confidence and energy to the interview are the two most important ingredients to connecting with the interviewer.

CHAPTER 9

The Summary

At this point, if you've been following along with the exercises, thinking about your stories, and building your inventory of stories, you have a good idea of how your new interview preparation method will help you present yourself as the ideal candidate for any job.

It's always good to review once you've accomplished your mission. The tools and techniques are summarized for you here to take one last look at before you try your hand at taking the quiz.

The Tools and Techniques of Interviewing

The 10 Most Common Key Factors

- **Honesty and integrity**: moral issues
  To be trustworthy; to avoid deceit; to present issues frankly and fully; to make the right decision at any cost, choosing between right and wrong

- **Communication:** relating to others, convincing others
  Oral: to speak concisely, grammatically correct, and in an organized manner; to be able to talk through problems with coworkers or customers; to negotiate situations in a calm manner; to follow instructions or directions; able to convince others to see things your way
  Written: to write in a manner that is concise, well-organized, grammatically correct, effective, and persuasive

- **Adaptable:** open to change, flexible
  A willing attitude; adjusts quickly to change; comfortable in new situations; willing to do what is asked; performs above and beyond what the job calls for

- **Problem solving:** analyze, evaluate, judgments/decisions
  To discern what is appropriate; to make good judgments and decisions; to deal with facts and evaluate, research, and explore options; to look at all aspect of situations before jumping to conclusions

- **Initiative:** above and beyond, resourceful
  To step forward; to formulate creative alternatives or solutions; to resolve problems thinking out of the box; to show flexibility in response to unanticipated circumstances

- **Leadership:** motivate, role model, team player
  To recognize and assume responsibility for work that needs to be done; to persist in the completion of a task; to influence group activity; to motivate others to participate in an activity

- **Plan and organize:** prioritize

  To prioritize and plan tasks effectively; to employ a systematic approach to achieving objectives; to make appropriate use of limited resources; to meet deadlines

- **Accountable:** results-oriented

  Ability to "make it happen"; to meet deadlines; to consistently follow through; to use resources available to achieve results; time management and prioritization; to know when to ask for assistance

- **Composure:** to stay positive

  To stay calm, poised, and effective in stressful or difficult situations; to think on one's feet; to adjust quickly to changing situations; to maintain self-control

- **Self-motivated:** enthusiastic, passionate

  Determined; ability to perform with little or no supervision; to make the most of what is available; to take the initiative and go above and beyond what is asked

The Three Categories of Skills, Abilities, and Traits

1. **Knowledge-based skills:** skills learned through experience or education

   Examples: computer programs/languages; graphics; writing skills; training skills; management experience; sciences: chemistry, biology; coaching skills, sales experience; leadership training; project management; operations; marketing; event planning; policy development; legal expertise; strategic planning; liaison; mediator; product management; research skills; business acumen; mechanically adept; and others.

2. **Transferable or general skills:** skills that can be thought of as "portable skills." You can take them with you to almost any job. They are broad-based and usually learned or acquired through experience.

    Examples: communication; listening; decision making; judgment; initiative; planning; organizing; time management; leadership; work ethic; interpersonal skills; common sense; social skills; creative ideas; sees big picture; analytical; accountable; reliable; high standards; resourceful; action-oriented; intuitive; problem solving; good with numbers; gets along well with others; articulate; handy; artistic; envisioning

3. **Personal traits:** qualities that make you unique. These traits can sometimes determine whether you are a good fit for the company, the department, or the position.

    Examples: dependable; strong; team player; versatile; patient; friendly; energetic; formal; loyal; self-confident; dynamic; practical; sociable; persuasive; responsible; sense of humor; cheerful; good attitude; aggressive; assertive; determined; honest; humble; productive; conscientious; curious; enthusiastic; precise; detail-oriented; compassionate; efficient; emotional; firm; open-minded

Interview Principles and Rules to Discuss Salary

The Basic Principles of Salary Negotiation

1. You can't negotiate anything until you have an offer. Don't go there yet.
2. Know your walk-away point—when you can't afford to take the offer.
3. Know the rules of salary negotiation before discussing salary.
4. Know what you want: the whole package and the priorities of wants.

The Seven Rules of Salary Negotiation

Rule One: He who mentions a dollar figure first, loses.

Rule Two: Never try to negotiate until you have an offer.

Rule Three: Do not accept on-the-spot offers.

Rule Four: Always get the offer in writing.

Rule Five: Keep it friendly.

Rule Six: Consider your position before making deals.

Rule Seven: Focus on the base salary first.

The Five-Point System

Writing out your five points will be extremely important to answering key questions about *you*.

Point One: Your education and years of experience

Point Two: Your area of expertise

Point Three: Your key strength

Point Four: Your work ethic or work style

Point Five: Personal facts

Using Your Fingers to Remember

The thumb (strong base): education and experience.

The pointer finger (directed): your expertise or knowledge of the job.

The middle finger (to the point): your strength—transferable or personal.

The ring finger (loyalty): people skills, communication, whatever it takes attitude.

The little finger (weakest): personal information that is engaging and interesting about you or how the combination of all these traits together makes you unique.

Your Examples and Stories

Behavioral Stories

Don't just tell; show the action.

"Tell me about a time..."

"Give me an example..."

"Describe a situation..."

Guidelines for Storytelling

- The beginning is 20 percent of the story.
- The middle is 60 percent of the story.
- The ending is 20 percent of the story.

Situational Thinking

"What would you do if…?"

A: The first thing I would do is to analyze.

R: Next, I would do research.

D: Then I would develop…

I: After that I would implement…

E: I always evaluate and reevaluate.

The Five Categories of Interview Questions

1. Who are you? What do have to offer?

2. Why do you want to work here?

3. Sensitive or negative questions.

4. What are your salary expectations?

5. Miscellaneous questions.

The Quiz

Okay, it's time to see if you've been reading and doing your homework. There will be a variety of questions to test your newfound knowledge.

The questions regarding factors can be answered using several factors, depending on the focus of the action in your story. For the benefit of this quiz, it will work best if you focus on the most obvious factor for now. Later when you begin to get the hang of choosing which factor works best, you can think of several factors to use.

To begin the quiz, read the question and determine the main factor the interviewer is seeking. Next, determine whether the question is a behavioral question that will require a story, or a situational question that will be answered by demonstrating how you would think through a problem. Also, think about the category the question falls under (one of the five categories of questions).

There are really no wrong answers, but the answers that apply can be found on the pages following the quiz. Rate yourself and see how you measure up as a candidate who can determine what the interviewer is seeking and then answer the question based on your prep work.

Let the quiz begin!

The Quiz

1. **Question: "Describe a time when you had a conflict with a coworker."**

   What factor is the interviewer seeking?
   Is this a behavioral, situational, or general question?
   Which of the five categories does this question fit?
   What skills, traits, or abilities are important to this answer?

2. **Question: "How would you plan and organize an event?"**

   What factor is the interviewer seeking?
   Is this a behavioral, situational, or general question?
   Which of the five categories does this question fit?
   What skills, traits, or abilities are important to this answer?

3. Question: "What steps do you take to fix a problem before it becomes a major problem?"

What factor is the interviewer seeking?
Is this a behavioral, situational, or general question?
Which of the five categories does this question fit?
What skills, traits, or abilities are important to this answer?

4. Question: "What is your strength?"

What factor is the interviewer seeking?
Is this a behavioral, situational, or general question?
Which of the five categories does this question fit?
What skills, traits, or abilities are important to this answer?

5. Question: "Why do you want to work for this company?"

What factor is the interviewer seeking?
Is this a behavioral, situational, or general question?
Which of the five categories does this question fit?
What skills, traits, or abilities are important to this answer?

6. Question: "How do you get others to buy into your goals and objectives?"

What factor is the interviewer seeking?
Is this a behavioral, situational, or general question?
Which of the five categories does this question fit?
What skills, traits, or abilities are important to this answer?

7. Question: "In your last position, what type of relationship did you maintain with other business departments?"

What factor is the interviewer seeking?
Is this a behavioral, situational, or general question?

Which of the five categories does this question fit?
What skills, traits, or abilities are important to this answer?

8. Question: "What salary range would you require to take this job?"

What factor is the interviewer seeking?
Is this a behavioral, situational, or general question?
Which of the five categories does this question fit?
What skills, traits, or abilities are important to this answer?

9. Question: "What are three words that describe you?"

What factor is the interviewer seeking?
Is this a behavioral, situational, or general question?
Which of the five categories does this question fit?
What skills, traits, or abilities are important to this answer?

10. Question: "Do you have any questions for me (the interviewer)?"

What factor is the interviewer seeking?
Is this a behavioral, situational, or general question?
Which of the five categories does this question fit?
What skills, traits, or abilities are important to this answer?

What to Say in Every Job Interview

Answers to the Quiz

1. Question: "Describe a time when you had a conflict with a coworker."

   What factor is the interviewer seeking?

   Answer: The main factors would be communication and relating to people. The answer could also include other factors, such as staying calm under stress, or possibly taking the initiative, depending on the action in your story.

   Is this a behavioral, situational, or general question?

   Answer: This is a behavioral question that requires an example or story. When a question begins with a phrase such as: "Describe a time when...," you should think "past behavior" and know that to answer the question you need to have an example.

   Example of a behavioral answer to this question:

   Problem:

   There was a time when I had a conflict with a student of mine named Ellen. She was very disruptive in class by always making negative comments to herself and others and disturbing the other students. Some of the students came to me and expressed their concern about her. I knew I had to deal with the situation.

   Action—What I did was:

   I asked Ellen to stay after class so that we could talk. She immediately became defensive and started talking about how she was singled out and hadn't done any-thing. At one point she was yelling.

I stayed calm and told her that we could speak in a normal tone and she didn't need to yell. I asked her if there was any way that I could help her. Was she frustrated because she didn't understand the work?

I told her I was very available to her and that I was willing to meet with her to help her. Ellen began crying and said that she was sorry and that she was under a lot of stress about things that were happening at home.

I listened to her vent for about a half-hour, and then we discussed a possible tutoring plan solution to her frustration in class.

I also referred her to the school psychologist to discuss her problems with a neutral person.

Result:

The next time we had class she apologized to me and brought me an apple. After that things went much smoother. The tutoring plan worked, and she ended up passing the class with a higher grade than I had imagined. She came to me on the last day of class and thanked me and told me she would not forget what she had learned from our discussion and working together.

I reminded myself that this is why I teach.

Which of the five categories does this question fit?

Answer: This question is a negative or sensitive question of a time when things weren't going well with a coworker or a boss. Or, it could be a time when you had to handle a difficult situation.

What skills, traits, or abilities are important to this answer?

Answer: Important skills would be communication and being able to deal with difficult situations. These are primarily transferable skills that you could use in any position.

How do you rate yourself on your answers?

_____

Where do you still need some work to be prepared?

_____

2. **Question: "How would you plan and organize an event?"**

What factor is the interviewer seeking?

Answer: The main factor here is planning and organizing. It could also include problem solving, communication, and relating to others to organize any event.

Is this a behavioral, situational, or general question?

Answer: This is a situational question. The words "How would you…" indicate that it hasn't happened, but what if it did? What would you do?

Example of a situational answer to this question:

Analyze:

The first thing I would do would be to evaluate the scope of the event, who would be involved, what level of client would participate, and what my budget would be.

Research:

The next thing that I'd do is to begin research. What has been done in the past? What are my resources as far as other team members? What possible venues would work for the event? Who would be an experienced event planner to use as a resource?

Develop:

Once I had all the information I needed, I would put together a spreadsheet and set up files to plan the steps and the calendar of dates and deadlines. I would also develop a budget to make sure that I stayed within what had been allotted for the event. I would use any resources available to assist me in the development of a well-organized plan.

Implement:

When I felt the plan was in place and the steps were solid, I would roll out the plan and begin taking action steps. I would make sure that each team member was clear about his or her responsibilities and that the contact information for each person was available to all team members.

Evaluate:

Even though I had done a thorough job on details and schedules, I would constantly evaluate the event to ensure everything was running smoothly. Any changes that had to be made I would take care of personally to ensure that everything was in place.

Which of the five categories does this question fit?

Answer: This question falls under the "Who are you? Can you do the job? What do you have to offer?" category. The interviewer wants to hear how you think. Because it is a situational question, you do not have to give an example or story. If the question asked, "Tell me about a time when you organized an event," that would be a behavioral question, and would require an example.

What skills, traits, or abilities are important to this answer?

Answer: The skills to organize and plan are your ability to think in an organized manner, taking into account deadlines, budgets, resources, and leading teams. Most of these skills are transferable skills that you could use in any job.

How do you rate yourself on your answers?

_____

Where do you still need some work to be prepared?

_____

3.   Question: "What steps do you follow to study a problem and fix it before it becomes a major problem?"

What factor is the interviewer seeking?

Answer: The main factors would be problem solving, to evaluate and make decisions. The other factors to consider would be thinking creatively or "out of the box." And, in order to stop something from becoming a bigger problem, it would also require some forward thinking and ability to take action.

Is this a behavioral, situational, or general question?

Answer: This is a situational question. "What would you do if?" The interviewer wants to hear the logic behind your thinking process. Can you demonstrate thinking through a problem?

By using the ARDIE template, you can answer this question. You can use an actual situation when you solved a problem before it got out of hand. (Present as evaluating and making a decision).

Which of the five categories does this question fit?

Answer: The interviewer is listening for your problem solving ability to see if you can do the job. This question falls under the "Who are you? What do you have to offer?" category. It is almost impossible to prepare for situational questions other than to look at the factors involved. In this question, your evaluation and problem-solving thinking is where you should focus.

What skills, traits, or abilities are important to this answer?

Answer: Answering the situational question takes a certain ability to "think on your feet." So you are showing your ability not only to solve the problem (which is a transferable skill) but to come up with an answer quickly by being able to adapt (also a transferable skill).

How do you rate yourself on your answers?

_____

Where do you still need some work to be prepared for the interview?

_____

4.   **Question: "What is your strength?"**

What factor is the interviewer seeking?

Answer: This answer will depend on what you consider to be your strength. "Who are you?"

If you wrote out your five points you will know your key strength right away. If your strength is in line with something the job description states as necessary or desired, this is a good time to talk about your strength as a match for the position.

Is this a behavioral, situational, or general question?

Answer: This is a general question about you. "Tell me about yourself, and what you have to offer."

Example of a good answer:

One of the qualities I pride myself on is my ability to protect information, particularly confidential

*information. My last boss would tell you he trusted
me with his personal information as well as his top
secret business information.*

The reason this is a good answer:

If confidentiality is high on the list of requirements for
the position you are going for, you have let the interviewer
know that this is something you excel in. Using a quote or
paraphrasing what your last boss would say is another way of
letting the interviewer know something about you without
actually saying it yourself. By saying, "My boss would say..."
you are using a third party endorsement to make your statement stronger.

This could also be used as an example of honesty and
integrity (transferable skills).

Which of the five categories does this question fit?

Answer: Although this is definitely a "Who are you?" question, it could also be a sensitive question if you don't like
bragging about yourself. Writing out your five points will
provide a resource to draw from that will make you feel more
comfortable. Talking about yourself as though you were a
product with certain qualities will feel much more natural.

What skills, traits, or abilities are important to this answer?

Answer: Keeping in mind what the job description says.
Your answer will depend on what the job description is
asking. Once you have identified where you are a strong
candidate when considering the requirements of the job,
it will be easier to answer questions about you without
feeling like you are "tooting your own horn."

More than likely, your strength is a transferable skill, unless you have a niche in which you are an expert or have outstanding skills. In that case, your knowledge-based skill may be your strength.

How do you rate yourself on your answers?

_____

Where do you still need some work to be prepared for the interview?

_____

5. **Question: "Why do you want to work for this company?"**

What factor is the interviewer seeking?

Answer: Your answer should include some company information and why you want this particular job at this particular company. A few of the factors that would be demonstrated in your answer here are your motivation and your enthusiasm or passion. If there are two equal candidates, the one that appeared more motivated and passionate about what the company does could be the one to tip the scale in her direction.

Example of an enthusiastic answer:

What I know about this company and your vision for employees matches exactly with the kind of company that I am looking to join. I did some in-depth research and was impressed by the growth and the management behind the growth. I was very impressed with the latest acquisition the company made, and I see this as a prime opportunity. I am looking beyond what I do at my current company to advance when I am ready and someday move into a management position. I know it will take time and hard work, but I am ready and willing to do whatever it takes.

The reason this is a good answer:

It gives you an opportunity to demonstrate your knowledge of the company, either through research or having dealt with them as a consumer. A little flattery goes a long way, even when it's about a company or product.

Is this a behavioral, situational, or general question?

Answer: This is a general question that attempts to determine whether you are going for just any job, and may leave the company when things improve, or if you are really motivated by the company and what it is they provide.

Which of the five categories does this question fit?

Answer: This falls under Category Two, "Why do you want to work here?" It's an important question that you should be prepared to offer in a positive manner. Just as they want to know if they like you and whether you will fit in, you also should be determining whether you like them and whether you would fit in.

What skills, traits, or abilities are important to this answer?

Answer: One of the challenges of interviewing is being yourself. If you are not known for being "enthusiastic," it may be difficult for you to show enthusiasm or passion in the interview. In that case, rely on facts as your answer. Example of an answer that relies on facts vs. passion:

The first reason is because of your position in the mar-
ket. The second reason is that I believe in the research
you are performing. And, thirdly, I have checked out
various sources, and this company has a good reputa-
tion. I would like to work here.

These are personal traits, and each person has his or her
own way of expressing what he or she believes or feels.

How do you rate yourself on your answers?

_____

Where do you still need some work to be prepared for the
interview?

_____

6.   **Question: "How do you get others to buy into your
     goals and objectives?"**

What factor is the interviewer seeking?

Answer: This question would pertain more to the management or executive level. The interview is looking for
an ability to be a leader, to motivate, to be a role model.
The factors would be to assume responsibility and to
influence others through motivation.

Is this a behavioral, situational, or general question?

Answer: The question is somewhere between a behavioral
and a situational question. When an interviewer asks a
question about "How did you do it," it indicates that you
have done this in past roles and it is a behavioral question

requiring a story or example. If the question was: "How would you get others to buy into your goals and objectives?" then the question would be a situational question that would require a thinking process rather than a past experience. Listening carefully to what the interviewer is asking would be very important here to give the strongest answer.

Example of a good behavioral answer:

My focus is on results. Recently, my team committed to a goal of increasing profits by 25 percent before the end of the quarter. I met with my team and set very specific objectives. I was able to get their individual commitment. We agreed they would receive a percentage of profits upon completion of the goal. I personally committed, and was held accountable, to the board of directors. We worked as a team to achieve a very successful campaign. Communication was the key: knowing what the outcome should be and prioritizing work to that end. We were able to meet the goal in spite of a tight deadline.

The reason this is a good answer:

First of all it is a specific example: a story of a time when . . . Secondly, it gives quantitative results. This is a good example of past success as an indicator of what you can do in the future.

Which of the five categories does this question fit?

Answer: The question is asking about you and whether you can lead others. The category is: "Who are you? What do you have to offer?"

What skills, traits, or abilities are important to this answer?

Answer: The basis of the success is communication. The question is asking if you can motivate others, but the transferable skill is communication. Learning to motivate others through education and experience is more of a knowledge-based skill. Both skills, communication and motivation, are key to answering this question.

How do you rate yourself on your answers?

_____

Where do you still need some work to be prepared for the interview?

_____

7. **Question: "In your last position, what type of relationship did you maintain with other business departments?"**

What factor is the interviewer seeking?

Answer: The main factor would be your ability to communicate and relate to others. But this question is looking for something beyond communication, and that is how you deal with people outside your immediate circle. How do you reach out and build a relationship? In the management area this could be the ability to see the big picture perspective.

Is this a behavioral, situational, or general question?

Answer: This is about your "past" behavior, and even though it doesn't ask for an example, it is really asking: "Tell me about a time when you maintained relationships with other business departments."

Example of a weak answer:

I had many relationships with various business departments in the organization, and all of them were good.

Example of a stronger answer (a behavioral story):

My last position allowed me the opportunity to interface with almost every business department in the company. Because we had global locations this was not always easy.

What I did was set up a calendar and schedule, allowing for the various time zones, and I made sure I had weekly online meetings with each business department.

The most challenging part of this endeavor was being there at all hours of the day and night. This took some strategic planning on my part. I had many sleepless nights.

However, it really paid off. I was able to get to know each member of the different business departments, and they came to trust me in a way I couldn't have achieved without making the extra effort.

As a result, the business departments in every location not only felt included in the project work, but they turned out to be key contributors. I was given many kudos for going above and beyond in my projects.

Which of the five categories does this question fit?

Answer: The category is "What do you have to offer?" or "Can this candidate do the job?"

This is a question that is testing your ability to work with teams and motivate through example. The more specific your answer is, the greater the proof that you know how to build relationships and you are willing to do whatever it takes to do that.

What skills, traits, or abilities are important to this answer?

Answer: The ability to build relationships and motivate others is a knowledge-based skill, learned from education and experience. This can also be considered a personal trait, the ability to connect with a diverse group of people and find common interests.

How do you rate yourself on your answers?

_____

Where do you still need some work to be prepared for the interview?

_____

8. **Question: "What salary range would you require to take this job?"**

    What factor is the interviewer seeking?

    The factor the interviewer is interested in is how you handle this question. A key factor in some positions is negotiation skills. Being able to communicate and relate with others is a part of good negotiation. It is also part of being able to discuss difficult subjects. A discussion about money is by far the most difficult subjects to talk about, especially in an interview. You may come across as passive in your answer by saying something like: "Whatever you offer, I'm sure it will be a fair rate." Or, you may be straightforward. Either way, being prepared will make it easier for you to sound confident and comfortable with the discussion.

Is this a behavioral, situational, or general question?

This is more of a general question, but it has to do with the concern: "Can we afford this candidate?"

Which of the five categories does this question fit?

The category is clearly, "What are your salary expectations?" When you prepare you can give a strong answer.

Examples of answers:

Answer 1:

From the research that I have done it appears to be in the $60,000 to $70,000 range. Is that the range you had in mind?

(This is a good answer if they insist on a figure from you.)

Answer 2:

Based on my previous experience and education and the "going rate" for this type of position, I would like to be in the mid- to high 70s. Does that range fit in your compensation structure?

(Good answer if pushed for a figure—give an acceptable range.)

Answer 3:

I would need to know more about your salary structure and how often you review salaries as well as your

entire package before I could discuss salary ranges.
Could you provide me with more information before
we discuss this subject?

(Good answer to push back the discussion to the interviewer.)

What skills, traits, or abilities are important to this answer?

This is a very uncomfortable topic for most people to deal with in general. In an interview it is twice as stressful. Being able to stay composed under the pressure of this conversation will demonstrate not only your communication skills, but your ability to handle difficult situations.

How do you rate yourself on your answers?

_____

Where do you still need some work to be prepared for the interview?

_____

9. **Question: "What are three words that describe you?"**

What factor is the interviewer seeking?

The factor is your ability to know the factors that are important to the job and to be able to adapt and to communicate those factors in words that you would use to describe yourself. The first thing to determine is what the key factors are for this job. You should then be able to use one of the key factors to describe yourself. If a key factor is being able to adapt, you should be able to communicate this factor as one of your three words. "Adaptable." Only, of course, if this is true, because the next question may be, "Tell me about a time when you had to adapt to a new situation quickly."

Is this a behavioral, situational, or general question?

This is a general question that would be part of your five point preparation. You can easily draw from the work you've done to describe who you are when you wrote your five points.

Which of the five categories does this question fit?

The category is "Who are you? and "What do you have to offer." If you have prepared using the exercises in this book, you will be able to answer this question without a problem.

Examples of Three Words

Answer 1:

Reliable, friendly, and thorough.

This is not a good answer. You need annotation or examples of why you chose those words.

Answer 2:

"Hardworking" is the first. Anyone I work with would tell you that I do whatever it takes to get the job done. Second is "team player" because I thrive in environments that are supportive and collaborative. And last is "knowledgeable" regarding accounting information. Through my education and experience I have a strong background in all phases of accounting.

The reason this is a good answer:

The one flaw in this answer is to say "hardworking." That happens to be the number one most common answer given to this question. But, this answer goes on to tell what makes you a hard worker.

What skills, traits, or abilities are important to this answer?

Being able to talk about yourself without a false sense of modesty is a skill that you will have to work on if you want to impress the interviewer. This is not about bragging. It is about being able to communicate what you have to offer in a comfortable manner. This would be both a learned, knowledge-based skill as well as a personal trait.

How do you rate yourself on your answers?

_____

Where do you still need some work to be prepared for the interview?

_____

RULE OF THUMB

Never answer a question with a single word.

10. Question: "Do you have any questions for me (the interviewer)?"

What factor is the interviewer seeking?

The factor will be determined by the questions you ask. Certainly oral communication skills, but also some evaluation skills if you have been listening to what the interviewer has said and then reflected back with some questions about what you've heard. It is important for you to ask questions about the job to show that enthusiasm and passion.

Is this a behavioral, situational, or general question?

This is a general question that is seeking information from the interviewer. Some managers and interviewers are on the alert to just what questions you will ask, and where you will focus your attention.

Which of the five categories does this question fit?

This questions falls into the miscellaneous questions category, covered in Chapter 8.

It is a good idea to have questions ready or at least some thoughts about what you want to know about the company and the job based on your research. Be sure and go to the company's website and read as much as possible about the company mission and culture, as well as the responsibilities of the job.

What skills, traits, or abilities are important to this answer?

This is clearly a communication skill, but this time it calls on your listening skills as well as your ability to express yourself. Most people underestimate the importance of listening during the interview. If you are so focused on the questions and how you will answer, you might just miss some important clues that you will need to ask intelligent questions, and later on to decide if you will accept an offer.

How do you rate yourself on your answers?

_____

Where do you still need some work to be prepared for the interview?

_____

APPENDIX
Salary Information Resources

General Salary Surveys and Collections

Salary.com

(http://www.salary.com)

Much more than just salary resources, this site is dedicated not only to salaries, but also to total compensation. The Salary Wizard is fast and easy to use, allowing you to search for base, median, and top-level earnings in hundreds of jobs for many occupational areas, and much of the data is spun to your local jurisdiction. Beyond the Salary Wizard, you'll find helpful articles and exercises to help you figure out things like benefits, stock options, bonuses (and how to get them), and even negotiations.

Salary.com now offers you the opportunity to purchase a Personal Salary Report. This is a customized report targeted to your local market, your current level of experience, and the industry in which you work. It's also filled with tips and pointers you can use to help you with negotiations and raise requests.

Riley Guide

(http://www.rileyguide.com/salguides.html)

Finding salary information to help you make a decision or negotiate for better pay is not easy. There's the problem of finding up-to-date and reliable data for your situation. Then there's the problem of deciding if the data you are looking at is relevant to your situation. Finally, you have to know how to use the information you've found wisely in negotiations, should that mean asking for a raise or asking for a different (usually better) compensation package when accepting a new job.

This site has the largest collection of salary surveys online anywhere. Use these to find out how your current compensation rate compares with others in your area. However, be careful not to take this information as fact. Many factors combine to make up the actual pay rate offered by an employer.

JobStar Salary Surveys

(http://jobstar.org/tools/salary/index.php)

Originally established for the California job seeker, this site has the largest collection of salary surveys online anywhere. Combined with lists of books to request from your local library and articles from experts, this site will lead you in the right direction for your salary search.

SalaryExpert.com

(http://www.salaryexpert.com)

This website offers free access to extensive international compensation information prepared by extremely knowledgeable experts. The Basic Salary Reports for the United States and Canada or the International Salary Report cover many other countries, and each allows you to select a job title and region and returns a nice report showing salary averages, salary levels, benefits, and cost of living information.

Other premium, customized reports are available for a moderate fee, including the Premium Salary Report, The Executive Compensation with Comparables Report, and the U.S./Canada Employee Benefits Report.

Abbott, Langer & Associates

(http://www.abbott-langer.com)

Current salary survey statistics are available here for hundreds of benchmark jobs in high-tech, marketing/sales, accounting, engineering, human resources, consulting, manufacturing, nonprofit, legal, healthcare, and other fields from 8,000 participating firms and millions of OCR, digitized, incumbent, web-service, job boards, field job analyses, and other inputs.

Economic Research Institute

(http://www.erieri.com/index.cfm?FuseAction=FreeAnalyst Resources.Main)

Free compensation and job analysis resources are available through this compensation and benefits research organization.

Government Wage Surveys

The U.S. Bureau of Labor Statistics

(http://www.bls.gov/bls/wages.htm)

The U.S. Bureau of Labor Statistics collects all kinds of data on wages, unemployment, and other employment trends. Search through their press releases, regional data, and other areas for salary and compensation information.

Occupational Employment Statistics

(http://stats.bls.gov/oes)

Program produces employment and wage estimates annually for over 800 occupations. These estimates are available for the nation as a whole, for individual states, and for metropolitan and non metropolitan areas; national occupational estimates for specific industries are also available.

Government Reports and Survey

(http://stats.bls.gov/oes)

Use the Occupational Outlook Handbook and individual state labor market information pages to look for prevailing compensation for various occupations.

Other Ideas and Resources

Still not finding what you want or need? Try these resources.

Career and Occupational Guides

(http://stats.bls.gov/oes)

Most career and occupational guides include some broad references to expected earnings for each field or discipline discussed.

Professional and Trade Associations and Labor Unions
(http://www.rileyguide.com/union.html)

These organizations frequently survey their members to collect salary and wage information, and many trade associations and unions maintain standard pay rates for their local organizations. If you cannot find information on their websites, contact the office or local organization nearest you.

Career.Builder.com
(http://www.cbsalary.com/?sc_cmp2=js_home_cbsalary)

This site provides an easy tool with which to search salaries for thousands of jobs. Compare your job salary to that of your peers with a quick salary search. Then, you can complete a salary survey to customize your salary report based on your experience and education level. The customized salary report will show you a salary comparison of your salary and the average salary range for that specific job.

Index

About the Author

Carole Martin is an expert on interviewing and salary negotiation for the candidate as well as the interviewer. She speaks at conferences, business meetings, and classes. In addition to publishing many articles on websites and in publications, she has authored seven books on the subject of interviewing and hiring (five are published by McGraw-Hill): *Interview Fitness Training*, *Boost Your Interview IQ*, *Boost Your Interview IQ*, 2nd Edition, *Perfect Phrases for the Perfect Interview*, *Boost Your Hiring IQ*, *Perfect Phrases for Successful Job Seekers* (coauthor), and *Perfect Phrases for Writing Job Descriptions*.

Carole has more than 20 years of experience in human resources management in various industries including biotechnology, aerospace, software engineering, sales, publishing, and consulting. She is an acknowledged expert in the use of behavioral interviewing techniques and has made interviewing her specialty.

She has interviewed thousands of candidates at all levels in the corporate environment, as well as in academia and in nonprofit and government environments. She has many interesting stories and tips to pass along. Carole teaches her tips and techniques to job searchers and employers through one-on-one sessions, phone coaching, and group workshops. Thanks to the Internet, she has coached people across the United States and as far away as London, Paris, Israel, and China.